Life's 4th Quarter

Learn Live Give

By Joseph James Slawek

JOSEPH JAMES SLAWEK

Life's 4th Quarter

Copyright 2023 by Joseph James Slawek

Requests for information should be directed to:
Gina Capuani gcapuani@sfh71.com

ISBN 9798850882792

Cover design: Dan Yaeger, www.nu-images.com

All rights reserved. No part of this book may be reproduced or used in any manner without the prior written permission of the copyright owner, except for the use of brief quotations in a book review.

Printed in the United States of America.

For Mary

For our children and their spouses.

For our grandchildren, our great-grandchildren and their children.

And, for the many wonderful friends, colleagues and co-workers I've had the privilege of working alongside.

"One person's sunset is always another person's sunrise."

- Joseph James Slawek

TABLE OF CONTENTS

INTRODUCTION 1

OPENING PRAYER 4

WHAT DO I MEAN BY LIFE'S 4TH QUARTER? 5

The Parable Of The Bags Of Gold – The Sermon Of The Talents 9

Each According To His Ability 11

CHAPTER 1
LIFE's 1st QUARTER – EDUCATION 15

    The Road Leading Up 15

    Growing Up And Growing Within 17

    Finding Your Gifting 23

    A Note From Luke Slawek
    – Joe's Oldest Son 26

    Graduating To Q2 28

CHAPTER 2
LIFE'S 2nd QUARTER – CAREER LEARNING 31

Learning Your Industry And Business 31

Preparation To Create My Own Business 34

An Edge: Knowing Yourself 37

A Letter From Kirk Slawek 38

Leading By Influence, Not Control
– Purposeful Entrepreneurship.. 42

Graduating To Q3 — Lifelong Learning.................................... 43

CHAPTER 3
LIFE'S 3RD QUARTER – IN THE ZONE (EXCELLENCE)......... 45

Tenets Of Business And Life 45

Excellence Is Neither Perfection Or Mediocrity 46

Excellence Is The Persistent Pursuit Of Growth........................ 46

Failure Is A Good Thing 46

The CEO's Job... 48

Failing Forward.. 50

Perfection Is Impossible To Reproduce..................................... 52

The 2x4 Principle
– The Law Of Responsibility And The Principle Of Excellence... 54

A Note From Luke Slawek – Excellence 58

Life's 3rd Quarter Audit – An Accounting................................. 60

Graduating To Q4
— What Makes An "Excellent" 4th Quarter In Life? 67

CHAPTER 4
LIFE'S 4th QUARTER – GENERATIVE 69

The Time Is Now
– Genesis…A New Beginning 69

Beginning Life's 4th Quarter… 71

A Note From Mary 72

Genesis = Generative Generosity 76

A Note From Luke Slawek
– Continuing The Legacy 79

What's Next? 83

Fanfare For The Common Man 89

EPILOGUE 93
ACKNOWLEDGEMENTS 95

INTRODUCTION

So why am I writing this book?

I've entered the 4th quarter of my life and I realized a while back that there is only so much time left on my game clock – on anyone's for that matter. I decided I want to impart some of what I have learned or embraced and leave an anthology of sorts for my children, grandchildren, great-grandchildren and my friends. I want to honor all that God has given me, whether that is this time, my talents, my passion for a life's work and most specifically, the love for my family.

First, I think I'm a common man. I am a man who despite or because I am common, I have done uncommon things. This common man approach of beginning and growing throughout my days, leads me to believe that most people come to the same progression which I identify as what happens in the stages of life, reflected in timeframes or experiences. I've classified them as:

- Life's 1st Quarter – Education
- Life's 2nd Quarter – Career Learning
- Life's 3rd Quarter – In the Zone (Excellence)
- Life's 4th Quarter – Generative

As in life, there is a flow to a book and in this one that flow is reflected in said quarters as chapters. Somewhat like football, basketball or business 'quarters', the experiences within each quarter overlap. Yet, I have compartmentalized the storytelling a bit so you can see a trajectory or roadmap.

In the creation process, it occurred to me that in each quarter we have Dreams, and we have Loves, and we have Mentors. I begin to ask, "In the quarters of your life, who do you love and what do you dream? If we all pursue our loves, do we have to sacrifice our dreams? What guides us? Who mentors us?"

I began to think about the sacrifices sometimes made. Maybe even how would life be different now if different choices were made. This experience or perhaps wisdom, informs life's 4th quarter because choices and decisions are still coming. It's a perpetual assessment of what drives you and on what principles are you guided.

Before I even define 'here' in my 4th quarter, we will take a trek down multiple lanes of Quarters 1, 2 and 3. This path—or these paths—will offer the breadcrumbs or 'paper trail' so to speak, leading to the tale of how and why I am who I am, let alone where I am on my God led journey.

Upon entering life's 4th quarter a lot of us, especially those of us who are Baby Boomers, look for significance. I am not an exception. Writing *Life's 4th Quarter* is an opportunity to have significance with grandchildren, with great-grandchildren, with friends, with peers, and with others. As I reflect on what I've created and been given, the significance of it still lies in what I do with it.

My hope is that any wisdom and knowledge I have accumulated is imparted here and serves another. I will touch on some of the usual suspects in a book such as leadership, overcoming obstacles, definition of success and most importantly I will convey the importance of faith. My intention is to share what got me 'here' and a little bit of how.

We will hone in on what a great – an excellent – 4th quarter looks like. As you will read, the primary focus at this point is generative, in the planting of seeds in new generations. Generosity is the genesis of it. Life's 4th quarter is a new beginning (actually, each quarter offers a new beginning). Being generative and behaving generously are important to me, critical even. In the generative space, perhaps what I know will be perpetuated. In generosity, there is no expectation of receiving a return. It is giving for the sake of being able to do so, being able to bless the life of another. It suggests no exchange.

I may never meet who I am able to touch. As my wife, Mary, says, "That is an honor…a blessing." Mary, who has been my support across the ups and downs of many years, is and has always been at the forefront of continuing our journey of blessing.

As mentioned, a resounding reason for my writing this book is to be able to present it to my children, my grandchildren and great-grandchildren. And this book might sit on a shelf—until the exact moment it is needed. I envision someday bearing witness in the Kingdom, to hearing, "Oh, this is the book my father (or my grandfather or my friend) wrote. Maybe it will say something to me that I need today."

I envision fingers touching the book's spine as it is removed from its holding place and a page opens with a phrase that speaks to a beloved reader. An unknown memory or passion becomes known. A nugget of advice is taken in. A knowing that the author cared for me that much to share of his depths. An imprint on a heart and maybe a soul, is made.

At that point, I would hope to hear, "Well done, my good and faithful servant" from Matthew 25.

Enjoy *Life's 4th Quarter*. Enjoy the journey to reach your life's 4th quarter. I pray the contents I convey offer a vessel to transport you to success and significance on your path.

With love and God's grace.

OPENING PRAYER

Thank you, God.

I never thought I'd make it this far.

And here you put me in this wonderful, super-abundant spot where I have my family, my children, a good name and reputation.

…On to a new beginning.

My Life's 4th Quarter.

WHAT DO I MEAN BY LIFE'S 4TH QUARTER?

"There is only so much time left on my personal game clock.

This is an exciting time as a new beginning.

The 4th Quarter of life is an amazing opportunity.

AND, I get a full quarter to do it!"

- Joseph James Slawek (JJS)

I intend to finish well. What I have learned across my years and experiences, is that the excellence I continue to aspire to requires conscious thought, planning and preparation. It also includes a generous amount of planting and sowing new seeds while learning from and applying knowledge and understanding from the prior harvests.

When I was younger, I had a mentor who was my partner in the business, Flavors of North America (FONA). As Aldo neared retirement age, he used a remark that stuck with me. His face would light up and he'd say, "Hey, Joe, I'm going into the 4th quarter!"

Aldo was the originator of my life's 4th Quarter thinking. He helped me to understand that the 4th Quarter in life isn't necessarily retirement, but an opportunity to pass along what I have learned and accumulated

– especially what I learned.

The next question? What will you do with that time?

After much deliberation and preparedness/readiness, I've sold FONA International, the company I (and my family/team) built, though I do not intend to 'finish working' or retire. I don't even like the word 'retire', but I'll use it in the book for context.

Life's 4th Quarter is not a time to sit back. It is a time to continue. It is also a time to further honor and know God's view vs. the desk view. Being a steward does not stop in the last quarter. And in my case and hopefully many others', it requires focus on faith, family and fun.

I've earned the income and the good reputation and name and now I have graduated to this new beginning. There is much more I want to do and plan to do for people with the assets and learning accumulated. And, gratefully, because of many levels of success, there is much more I can or must do.

I see this time of life as A New Beginning.

What led up to this perspective?

Philosophically, I began to think of my life in quarters and embraced introspection on the quarters reflecting patterns in everyone's life. In essence, if we look at lifespan, we can chalk it up to four quarters as follows:

LIFE'S 1ST QUARTER: EDUCATION

The 1st Quarter in life was almost exclusively education – that education from kindergarten through college was basically a 20-year process. (I don't think the years are important, but for the fact that it took the first quarter of my life to hone basic skills.) In this quarter, you are a full-time student and a part-time worker.

I dreamt of a college degree – a 'union card' to a better job and a better income.

As for love in Q1, there is a relatively narrow love group – self, family and if you are fortunate like me, the love of your life – in my case, my wife, Mary.

My mentors were mostly in the form of parents, teachers, bosses and other relatives.

LIFE'S 2ND QUARTER: CAREER LEARNING

The task of the 2nd Quarter of life becomes learning the game, so to speak, and how to play to your position. You might be in or approaching your thirties. You've switched it up to full-time work and part-time education. You are still learning skills and how to best do your job and likely if you do not learn both you will not stay in that industry. Hopefully during that time, you find a series of increasing challenges and successes.

I dreamt of how to be the most highly compensated. (I explain the salary 'scorecard' in a bit.)

I developed a love of business and customers, as well as a love of co-workers.

This quarter is when I began understanding what it meant to be sacrificial. Gratefully, my guidance grew, as Mary and I were saved as Christians.

My mentors were my industry leaders and those who helped me to learn and excel in my role, profession and industry.

LIFE'S 3RD QUARTER: IN THE ZONE (EXCELLENCE)

Now you know your industry, your job and a bit more about yourself. You've hit your stride and are in your zone. Your work isn't work, as much as it is just what you do with more wisdom and focused performance.

You've pretty much become the CEO of your life. The question is: "How good do I want to become?" While you are always learning, it is now about execution. It's about excellence.

I dreamt of being excellent – and to live that kind of excellence every single day.

I love that love expands and I have more love with my children and spouse. Also, I love that I am led by Christian business principles.

Mentorship came in the form of scripture, faith-based leaders and best in industry professionals.

LIFE'S 4TH QUARTER: GENERATIVE

This is the 'real' new beginning – the time to plant the seeds for new generations. Being generative is paying it forward.

It is true that a grateful and indebted heart reflects a generous spirit. What better time to be generous with all that God has given me, than through my life's 4th quarter.

I dream of how I might be remembered by my children, grandchildren and eventually by my great-grandchildren.

I love seeding the next generation, which includes time with my children, grandchildren and friends and more time with Mary. It also includes investing in generosity for those I may never meet.

At this point, you may ask, "Who are your mentors now?" What am I guided by? I suppose now, I have enough awareness and personal insight to know about that – as I continue growing in God.

I know I have learned from the first three quarters of my life and look forward to what is being created and will be created in the 4th quarter as a new beginning. Perhaps this nature of striving for excellence and the intensity that comes with it is why I love the following parable.

THE PARABLE OF THE BAGS OF GOLD – THE SERMON OF THE TALENTS

Matthew 25: 14-3- (NIV)

What does the common man need to know?

As my family, co-workers and colleagues will attest, one of my favorite parables in the Bible is in Matthew 25. It is called the sermon of the talents. I've spoken and written about it often and believe in Kingdom Economics and the 2x4 principle, reflected also in my previous work, titled, *The Ingredients for Success: The 10 Best Practices for Success*. More on that to come. For now, read the parable below:

> Again, it will be like a man going on a journey, who called his servants and entrusted his wealth to them. To one he gave five bags of gold, to another two bags and to another one bag, each according to his ability. Then he went on his journey. The man who had received five bags of gold went at once and put his money to work and gained five bags more. So also, the one with two bags of gold gained two more. But the man who had received one bag went off, dug a hole in the ground and hid his master's money.
>
> After a long time the master of those servants returned and settled accounts with them. The man who had received five bags of gold brought the other five. "Master," he said, "you entrusted me with five bags of gold. See, I have gained five more."
>
> His master replied, "Well done, good and faithful servant! You have been faithful with a few things; I will put you in charge of many things. Come and share your master's happiness!"

The man with two bags of gold also came. "Master," he said, "you entrusted me with two bags of gold; see, I have gained two more."

His master replied, "Well done, good and faithful servant! You have been faithful with a few things; I will put you in charge of many things. Come and share your master's happiness!"

Then the man who had received one bag of gold came. "Master," he said, "I knew that you are a hard man, harvesting where you have not sown and gathering where you have not scattered seed. So I was afraid and went out and hid your gold in the ground. See, here is what belongs to you."

His master replied, "You wicked, lazy servant! So you knew that I harvest where I have not sown and gather where I have not scattered seed? Well then, you should have put my money on deposit with bankers, so that when I returned I would have received it back with interest."

"So take the bag of gold from him and give it to the one who has ten bags. For whoever has will be given more and they will have an abundance. Whoever does not have, even what they have will be taken from them. And throw that worthless servant outside, into the darkness, where there will be weeping and gnashing of teeth."
– Matthew 25:14-30 (NIV)

EACH ACCORDING TO HIS ABILITY

So what does this sermon of the talents reflect?

We have all been entrusted with responsibilities to be cared for. This is an all-encompassing, very inclusive fact—EVERYONE has been entrusted gifts, property, family, friends and talents. Some people have more talent in a certain area than others. Some people have been given more talents and gifts in a particular area.

Matthew 25 says some were given five talents. Some were given two talents. Some were given one talent. We may have five talent CEOs and two talent CEOs. It is the same with employees and with our children. Whether we have been gifted in sports, business, cooking, teaching, studying or sewing—we each have responsibility to apply and grow our talents and gifts according to our abilities. As mentioned, I see myself as a common man – an ordinary guy with some extraordinary gifts. As such, I embrace my responsibility to grow the gifts of which I have been entrusted.

Because we each have unique gifts, we are all on our way to being somewhere better (and a better or improved version of ourselves in the process). This is most definitely a TRUTH and a REALITY in our 4th quarter of life. It is also our responsibility—and opportunity—to continue to grow from our lessons and extend a hand and a torch to assist and propel the growth of others.

I have often called myself a two talent CEO and I am grateful to be one. Since selling FONA, I no longer have the title of CEO. Well, not in a formal sense, though I am still the CEO of my own life. Now, it is my opportunity to strive toward being a five talent Good and Faithful Servant.

This includes how I distribute my faith, enjoy every moment with my family and continuously learn more about myself. Growth does not stop in life's 4th quarter. I'll reiterate throughout this writing, that it is a new beginning.

GOD'S RECYCLING PROGRAM

In business unused talent would cause customers to be taken away. In life, you could lose more than that. I think of the redistribution of unused talents as God's recycling program. You use your talents or you lose them. In life's 4th quarter, as with previous quarters, my intention is to use my talents and to continue to double them—to keep walking so to speak. This serves me and those whom I serve since the idea is also for those around me to double their talents.

In essence, my talents will be recycled through those to whom I pass them along.

No doubt, fear and uncertainty will be encountered. In Matthew 25, the man with the one gold bag experienced fear. I imagine the man with two bags and the man with five bags experienced fear too. Fear is not always a bad thing. It can be a motivator. It can, however, also stop forward movement and create missed opportunity.

As Nelson Mandela reminds us, "I learned that courage was not the absence of fear, but the triumph over it. The brave man is not he who does not feel afraid, but he who conquers fear."

We address uncertainty and fear by asking good questions like, "Who am I now? What's expected of me? What do I expect of myself? What's next?" And we seek clarity on those answers and our individual role in searching for and/or soliciting the answers. This is not the time to be a bystander, but an active participant.

If you don't attend to them and grow them, the talents you were given and those you have accumulated will, in fact, be redistributed. Use it or lose it, right?

I am delighted with what I have learned over the years and I have set in motion how to stay in motion whether when together with my family, having lunch with 'old' colleagues or in a great intellectual conversation. I plan to keep walking literally and figuratively.

Experience enjoyment in defining your life's 4th quarter. As Walt Disney says, "Tomorrow can be a very good age." And another wise soul advises, "If in doubt, look up."

Let's talk about in the beginning…Life's 1st Quarter…

CHAPTER 1
LIFE'S 1ST QUARTER – EDUCATION

THE ROAD LEADING UP

"God never calls the equipped. He equips the called."
- Joseph James Slawek (JJS)

"The more you read, the more you shall know. The more that you learn, the more places you shall go." - Dr. Suess

The first quarter in life's focus is almost exclusively education—that education from kindergarten through college, basically a 20-year process. Your education also shows up significantly on the home front and for some of us through part-time jobs too.

In Life's 1st Quarter, you are primarily about studying someone else's agenda—what the administrators and teachers are told to teach or think should be taught. I learned to read, write and do math and acquired technical, emotional and societal adeptness (I'd like to think). It's what you learn, fundamentals of education, which can differentiate any person going into the professional workplace.

However, finding your gifting…needs to be a focus in this quarter. Often, that's not the case. What do you love? What are you good at? We will cover more on that in a bit.

In this chapter, I tell a few stories of what formulated my interest in autonomy and business and which formulated my sense of responsibility, leadership and faith.

GROWING UP AND GROWING WITHIN

As written earlier, in each quarter of life we identify with a dream (or dreams) and love (or loves). In the 1st quarter for me I was very earnest about earning what I call my educational 'union card'. I dreamt of the college degree that would lead to a great job. I didn't really care about being educated per se – that was simply a bi-product. I wanted to surpass a blue-collar life and getting into college and graduating I saw as that transition.

My loves during this quarter seem pretty simple, but when I think about it – were complex. I loved myself – but I really loved my family. I grew up in a big family and am the oldest of eight children with alcoholic father (and very busy mother). Thus, I had oversight of my siblings on occasion and some high expectations were placed on me. As you might imagine, finances were slim and I was to be a contributor. I was incentivized greatly by my role in earning my keep and helping my family. I took my responsibility seriously.

My mentors included an array of family members and teachers, each of whom added uniquely to the person I was becoming.

EARLY YEARS

Growing up on the Northwest side of Chicago I had my first glimpse of what I could do with the resources that I had been given. From my earliest recollection I was taught by my parents the importance of hard work, so it should come as no surprise that I was already a part of the workforce at the age of eight as the paper boy, faithfully delivering the *Chicago Daily News* every day.

With my entrepreneurial debut as a paperboy at age 8 and the 'collections man' at age 10, along with some yard mowing and other odd jobs, I developed the budding work ethic of a businessman. I learned the principles of planning ahead and a daily commitment to work.

Maybe I was a bit young to be throwing papers, but I got along just fine—with one major exception. Part of my route included a three-story apartment building that required me to get the paper delivered to each family on their first, second, or third floor balcony. The first and second story created no problems. I could throw those newspapers onto their balconies. But the third floor was the challenge. Try as I might, I just couldn't get those newspapers to land on the third-floor balconies. The truth was that I simply wasn't strong enough—yet.

It was frustrating at first, but I learned persistence and discipline. I also learned how to plan and prepare for that particular hurdle. I knew those third story balconies were going to require additional time in comparison to throwing the other papers and I adjusted accordingly. Being prepared allowed me more time to 'practice'. Before too long, I was a pro at third-story launches.

What a feeling of accomplishment!

AUTONOMY, FREEDOM AND RESPONSIBILITY

My boyhood paper route taught many valuable business principles. I learned that doing your job well could be followed by a reward. Upon receipt of my first monthly paycheck of $13.38, I jumped on my bike and peddled to Rosen's Drug Store, basically a welcome, old-fashioned malt shop on a warm day after hard work. What made that corner store so special to me was its soda fountain. The silver red-padded stools were on one side and all manner of ice cream treats on the other.

I bellied up to the black and white marble counter and said, "I'd like a strawberry malt, please." As the blender whirred, I could feel my mouth already watering in preparation for what I was about to receive. Hey, I earned it!

I can assure you, a strawberry malt never tasted as good as that one did that day. Why? Because I didn't need any of my parents' money to pay for it—I bought it myself with my own money. As I sucked on the straw, the thick malt fighting me every step of the way, I thought to myself, "This is the greatest feeling in the world! I don't have to ask my parents for the money to buy stuff, I can do it myself!"

I probably didn't even know the word at the time, but I was relishing my newfound state of autonomy and that made it so sweet. That strawberry malt was worth every penny of the thirty-five cents I was charged. I felt such freedom.

On an even more personal note, there was another contributing factor to my maturing into a two talent CEO. When I was twenty-four years old, I suddenly lost my mother to a blood clot that reached her heart. I took over a major portion of the responsibility for my seven younger siblings. One of my goals was to make certain that all of them would be able to attend college. I'm pleased to say that we achieved that goal for each and every child—including me.

My identity, values and principles were in formation, as was my faith.

COLLEGE, FAMILY AND JESUS AS MY SAVIOR

While in college I met a beautiful young woman who completely captured my heart. Her name was Mary. We grew in our relationship by spending a significant amount of time together. We were married in 1979. We are still married today and she is one of the greatest blessings in my life. In 1981, we had our first child, Luke. A few years later came Kirk and Joy was our surprise little girl five years following Kirk.

On the outside we seemed like the typical family, happy and carefree. But I still couldn't give an account of my life in any sort of manner that brought lasting peace. All of that changed in 1983. We weren't really looking for a big change, but it was right on the horizon.

Mary and I were invited by good friends to a conference in Portland, Oregon and we agreed to spend that time with them. Frankly, I don't remember much of anything from the business portion of the meeting. But what I do remember was that the weekend was life changing.

The group running the conference offered a non-denominational Sunday church service which we attended. As the speaker began to teach, I knew what we were hearing was a different Gospel than anything I had heard before.

Mary and I were both very proud of our Catholic heritage, but this presenter was explaining that we could never do enough good works to earn a place with God. No, the only way to make peace with God was to accept what the Lord Jesus did for us on the cross. He died to pay for all our wrongdoings and invites us to receive him as the One who saves us. In accepting Christ as personal Savior, we were guaranteed eternal life because it wasn't dependent on my deeds, but on the deed Christ accomplished on the cross.

Mary and I were quite moved by this person's simple presentation of the Gospel. I needed a Savior and his name was Jesus.

At the conclusion of the message, the speaker gave everyone in the room an opportunity to come to the front to receive Jesus as Savior. Without hesitation, Mary and I slipped out of our seats and went forward. I later learned that this was a good old-fashioned altar call. We willingly complied.

God firmly came and snatched us up, even though we weren't necessarily looking for him at the time. Things have never been the same since that day. The Lord has been affirming my faith for all these years and continues to do so.

When we returned home to the Chicago area, our neighbors Doug and Jane Gault, invited us to begin attending church with them at the Hawthorne Hills Community Church. We accepted their invitation and immediately started gobbling up the strong teaching from the Bible. Slowly, our involvement with our Catholic tradition faded out of our lives as our biblical foundation grew. This new church experience was centered on Jesus and the teaching of his Word. We were eating it up like a couple of starving peasants at the King's table.

Eventually, we ended up at Christ Community Church in St. Charles, Illinois near our home. We continue to support the ministry there. Now we live in Gallatin, Tennessee and worship at Crosspoint Church. We love how we learn the teachings of the Word.

WHY DO I SHARE THIS PART OF MY LIFE WITH YOU?

Because through my decision to accept Christ as Savior, I have answered the ultimate question regarding the accounting of life. I know I will one day stand before God to give that account for my life. I can say, with full assurance, that I belong to Jesus, so that God will not see me in all my sin, but rather will see Christ in all his glory.

The Apostle Paul put it this way: "For God made Christ, who never sinned, to be the offering for our sin, so that we could be made right with God through Christ" (2 Corinthians 5:21, NLT). Friend, that's the answer for the final accounting. Are you ready for that appointment? Do yourself a big favor by making that decision right now. This may be your personal altar call.

You'll be glad you did. Eternally glad.

FINDING YOUR GIFTING

In the Life's 1st Quarter chapter title, I used the word, Education. As noted, in K-12 we are studying other people's agenda, which includes what administrators and teachers are required to teach. As we enter college, we have required basic ed classes needed and then add our own choices. Trade schools offer more choice in choosing a vocation on which to focus and still require a specific agenda or syllabus to follow.

In any case, I don't know about you, but I did not like trigonometry, not sure I ever used it, though I'm sure some do. There is a lot of emphasis today on science, technology, engineering and math (STEM) and pursuing associated careers. In a world moving into robotics, virtual reality (VR) and artificial intelligence (AI), I can see why. However, this does not resolve the issue of simply not excelling or enjoying the associated classes.

Within education we must include finding your gifting. You will be educated throughout life in many ways. One of those ways is in the realization of your gifts and applying them accordingly. Think about the 5-talent man in Matthew 25. Maybe some of his gifts included fearlessness in taking risks or stepping into the unknown. Maybe he would have made a good investment banker, but perhaps not an engineer.

What school should show you, as well as your influencers—whether parent, mentor or other—is to keep a close eye on your gifts. Identify and develop them early on and cultivate them across time.

You—any person—are not standardized and certainly not defined by standardized tests. You should really do the things you are good at. If math is easy for you, it is no accident. If you don't love it, that's not an accident either. This is where it gets complicated. Path and purpose are unveiled…and conscious attention and awareness of growing into your sweet spot(s) will sustain you.

Finding your gifting is not limited to just the 1st quarter, but I think in the first quarter the educational tracks are forced upon you. And almost always the focus is on 'fixing' weaknesses, not what you are good at. We all need fundamentals of course, though there should be a very healthy balance of enjoying the class that is easiest for you instead of perpetually having to overcome what is difficult for you.

A good example is someone who struggles with organic chemistry. If that's the case, why pursue a career in that field? Another person may like business writing or statistics. Whatever the class or topic, your response, affinity for the content and your aptitude tell you something about who you are. Being smart is not just about an "A" grade. It is about being deliberate about defining what you enjoy—and what you do not. If you are good at something, it's an indicator of one of your gifts. It could be the skill set you continue to develop and through which you move smoothly into a career of your choosing.

Again, my worldview may be shaped a little differently because I lived in a period before grade inflation, which is the process of assigning a higher grade than deserved based on a variety of factors, including a school or teacher's performance criteria. I think in high school I was more of a B/B-minus or C/C-plus kind of student. (Back then, probably a grade of C would be today's B.)

But I had a gift that the other kids didn't have. I didn't mind working because as the oldest of eight kids I was accustomed to it. And I also probably benefited from a high IQ because school was kind of easy. Perhaps too easy to engage me to be excellent.

No matter the era, the point is, if it was easy to do the classes you like, it wasn't easy by accident. You were good at it and understood it—a natural. We often hear, "It just comes naturally to me."

Classes become easy for you, number one because you are motivated, you are curious and there is an incentive for you to do it. There's no incentive maybe to take a sales course if you're a technical person, but there's no incentive to take a technical course if you're a salesperson, if that makes sense. And so you develop a greater hunger for education when it's so much more focused as it pertains to your interests and what you are good at. This is especially true in the second quarter of life as you build on basic skills, practically apply them and realize true competence.

I am pleased to add the letter below from our oldest son Luke John Slawek. Luke is one of the very brightest people that I know.

A NOTE FROM LUKE SLAWEK – JOE'S OLDEST SON

I remember early in life that my dad was resolved that education is the best investment. I recall my private school costing as much as 1/3 of our household income while the business (FONA) was started. My dad would say, "Education is the best investment in life. No one can take it from you."

I found this perspective to be rare, yet powerfully true. This commitment to finding the best education started with private Christian grade school and carried through my professional education in flight school and college, followed by further international business studies at INSEAD. I am eternally grateful for these investments and purposefully deploy the same values and priorities with my kids today.

I became an employee of FONA at 15 years old as I longed to follow my father, learn from him and support his legacy. He had developed a following from the community for his extraordinary performance and wisdom, of which I would soak up everything he said.

My responsibilities grew as my experience, career education and performance track record expanded. I began to find that my education equipped me as a differentiator in problem solving and that value creation came naturally. I began to see why the excellent people I worked with also benefited from personal development.

At FONA, all of our employees were required to attend at least 40 hours of continuing education, including myself. The core programs were created to be inclusive of our manufacturing floor staff to the C-suite. We could share learning experiences and implement difference making ideas across the entire company. The investment in us was intentional in that my dad knew the value of a willing, able and growing culture developed through education and validated with performance.

We began to find that not everyone was willing to pursue additional education and thankfully, we became magnetic for the ones who were. We cultivated and realized a cultural mindset of prosperity in a society of scarcity. We had staff sponsored MBAs, professional accreditations for technical careers, ESL (English as a second language) and countless personalized programs.

In reflection, my dad provided gifts of education that when aggregated would be measured by decades, if not centuries. I am grateful and indebted for my personal education, the culture we experienced and the profound results generated.

Thank you, Dad! Thank you, Mom!

GRADUATING TO Q2

The skills learned in Life's 1ˢᵗ Quarter are what differentiate a person and as more skill accumulates, the aggregate continues into the professional workplace. Combine this with having a direct impact on your interpersonal relationships, leadership capacity and fortitude, and you may have the ingredients to formulate a vision of excellence.

As you begin in your workplace, your education includes learning on the job and taking required training. You can also stretch out and be the over-achiever who takes the initiative and is proactive in learning on your own. You'll begin to see that almost every business problem somebody has figured out. Like me at my starting point, I wanted the highest paying job which was in sales. So, I needed to learn how to sell. Fortunately, Dale Carnegie and other resources have cracked that code and you can pick up a course on basic or advanced sales skills and learn. You can find content available for any subject for that matter.

Yes, I wanted to be a salesperson because it paid the most…but not for the money. I loved the scorecard! The money happened to be how the scorecard was measured. But once I started my own business in 1987, FONA, that was the last day I worked. I didn't have a job after that. It was just what I did. It was me. It's now how I give back.

Do you 'work' now? Everyone should get to the spot where they are applying their gifting such that it just doesn't feel like work anymore. It is just what you do.

The Lord Jesus was not the only one in the scriptures to affirm the principle of the talents. Consider the words of the Apostle Paul: "There is one Lord, one faith, one baptism and one God and Father, who is over all and in all and living through all. However, he has given each one of us a special gift through the generosity of Christ." – Ephesians 4:5-7 (NLT)

I am different than you. You are different than me. This is the way God made us. Just because I can do certain things better than you does NOT mean that I am better than you. In the same way, your doing certain things better than me does NOT make you better than me. We're all just wired differently. It's the principle of the Bags of Gold or Sermon of the Talents at work.

And it's coming back to that common man – taking the ordinary to extraordinary...

CHAPTER 2
LIFE'S 2ND QUARTER – CAREER LEARNING
LEARNING YOUR INDUSTRY AND BUSINESS

*'Tell me and I forget. Teach me and I remember.
Involve me and I learn."*

– Benjamin Franklin

The task of Life's 2nd Quarter becomes learning the game, so to speak and how to play to your position. You are still learning skills and how to best do your job. Whether you are a young salesperson, a young entrepreneur, a young scientist, a young administrator, a young HR person…it really wouldn't matter.

I dreamt of how to be the most highly compensated, not for the love of money but for the scorekeeping. I realized a salesperson's compensation was a direct measurement of your value to your organization.

My thoughts and actions led me to learn what it takes to earn money – or earn the most money and be financially successful. I had a desire to shine in my industry, to lead others, to seek in myself the best. And, how you know you are a good salesman – or good at any job – is the money. It is the score.

I developed love of business and customers, as well as co-workers. If you don't love the business and your customers, it is unlikely your financial scorecard will be the relative size of your dream.

This quarter is when I had an understanding of what it meant to be sacrificial. A hard charging, goal-oriented work ethic meant long hours and time away from home and family.

I was mentored by many and specifically in the food industry I was mentored by President, Arthur T. Schramm at Food Materials where I worked in high school through college and up to this point in my career. I was also indirectly mentored, or at least learned from, my co-workers and even customers. I'd be remiss if I didn't indicate Mary's role herein too. She stood beside me through personal growth and change and often helped me see things from a perspective that I'd previously not seen.

What I learned in Life's 2nd Quarter is that I was blessed to learn all the aspects of the business.

NOW...TO LEARN

Most likely now in your thirties, the 2nd quarter is where you learn to play and to win the game. Lifelong Professional Learning becomes key. Before you were studying, but now you're actually learning in your career. You learn your company and industry (or you will move along or be moved along). You learn how to be on time for work. You learn how to stay late. You learn what to do extra to get ahead. You learn the basics of your industry and the basics of your performance. You learn what works and doesn't and occasionally and sometimes the hard way, you learn what to say and what not to say, to do and what not to do.

Hopefully during that time, you find a series of increasing challenges and successes.

In the 2nd quarter of life, much of it is on the job learning—whether in professional pursuits or in personal life. There is a lot of self-exploration and a lot of navigating change. From academics to gainful employment and promotion, to getting married and beginning a family, it is a lot to traverse. Mistakes are made and learned from and learned from again. No doubt, we all experience lifelong learning. We get to become much more involved in defining our agenda.

BETTER AGENDA. BETTER OUTCOME.

In the 2nd quarter of life, it's the first time you're really learning because you care about your job. Now I'm not saying that young people shouldn't change jobs if they don't like something. Sometimes you want to go into a certain field and discover, "Hey, I actually found out I liked management better." You begin to see natural passages that should occur.

The need for reassessment and self-discovery in life are nicely described in Gail Sheehy's book, *Passages: Predictable Crises of Adult Life:*

> "If we don't change, we don't grow.
> If we don't grow, we aren't really living."
>
> – Gail Sheehy

Matthew 25 talks about the elements of preparation, individual talents, giftedness and sportsmanship. We are entrusted by our Creator with certain gifts and talents, which we are required to grow. He puts them on loan to us and we have our choice to develop them, use them, or lose them.

This Q2 time period was pivotal in determining the trajectory of my life.

PREPARATION TO CREATE MY OWN BUSINESS

People do realize their dreams. I realized my 2nd Life Quarter dream. Early in my thirties, I found myself as the highest compensated salesperson at Food Materials, a flavor company I had worked at during high school, throughout college and full-time since graduation. Applying the effective use of planning and preparation, I learned everything I could about our customers' needs and consequently, I rose through the company.

Ultimately, I became the Assistant to the President, which became part of how I prepared to lead my own company (even though I didn't know it at the time). I learned by observing what a CEO must deal with on a daily basis. And it was becoming abundantly clear that based on what I had learned early at home and in my sales career, I enjoyed autonomy. As I continued to plan for my future, I experienced an ever-increasing desire for autonomy. It is not uncommon for men to go through that sort of phase, especially in their early to mid-thirties.

The more I pondered that desire, the more I sought counsel from those I respected, some of whom I call my adopted fathers. And the more I prayed for God's guidance, the more the same thought kept reverberating over and over in my brain: If I really want autonomy, I need to have my own business!

Well, so much for what I loved…I was becoming so successful at Food Materials that I found that co-workers who I had loved began cheering for my downfall, or at least a reduced compensation package. As you can imagine, it's a frustrating position to be in when your own management peers look for ways to reduce your compensation. If I started my own company, my performance would never be my own enemy. Just the opposite, it would lend great credence to guaranteeing my own success.

At the same time, I was experiencing growing awareness and interest in my spiritual life. For the first time in my life, I was fully realizing how much God cares about my business and about me. I thought there was a better way, I needed to do it that way—by starting my own company. It began with planning and preparation and putting together a strong team. I had a partner, Bill Bowring, who was going to run the sales department, so he and I began brainstorming all the aspects of creating a new company.

I was truly grateful to assist the President for those years at Food Materials, since that position required me to be on multiple planning and executive committees, providing a close-up view of what planning and preparation are all about. I had the opportunity to be mentored by then President, Arthur T. Schramm, who taught me about the industry and about what's involved in being president of a company.

I also saw that God had given me exposure to the entire operations of a flavor company.

Since FONA was planned while I was employed, I owed Food Materials the obligation of an honest day's work. Our entrepreneurial efforts were done on our own time, perhaps during a breakfast, lunch, or dinner—often sketched out on paper napkins.

The point is – we took action and a lot of it. Many talk about starting their own business, but how many do? Many think about it, but nothing happens. They don't begin. As for me, I was so passionate about having my own business that utilizing my own time or spare time didn't feel at all like a burden. I knew what I was working toward.

Nature, people and technology were key elements in our vision. Nature as the model for great flavors. People as the artists creating and delivering those great flavors. Technology as the means to extend our competitive advantage as a method. Our plans (we still have many of those napkins with sketches on them) often took the form of the question:

How do we _____? (Fill in the blank: incorporate, hire an accountant, hire an attorney . . .).

A great number of To Do checklists are also carried on said coffee-stained napkins.

In April of 1987, we pulled the trigger. I've often said in retrospect that pulling the trigger is the most difficult part of the entire process. One can dream, one can hope, one can pray, one can plan, but when it's go-time, there really are only a select few with the one-time surge of courage necessary to go all the way in the process.

Thinking of being in business for yourself is very different than being in business for yourself.

> "By three methods we may learn wisdom: First, by reflection, which is noblest; Second, by imitation, which is easiest; and third by experience, which is the bitterest."
> – Confucius

Some people would say it was very risky, at the age of thirty-seven, to leave a very lucrative and secure position and take an 80 percent pay cut. In fact, I was suddenly making about the same money I had previously been paying in taxes. I really believed, however, that there was an opportunity for a small, independent, excellent, service-oriented and highly technical company.

Gratefully, I was right.

AN EDGE: KNOWING YOURSELF

Knowing yourself, your strengths and your temperament can help you to be prepared in business or life. This knowledge will help shape your goals. To either fail forward or achieve at greater levels, I needed to know more about myself and how I showed up in the world in my eyes and the eyes of others. As Shakespeare wrote, "To thine own self be true." It helps if you know quite a bit about 'thine own self'.

How wonderful for someone to say, "I like what I am and I'm going to be more of what I am." This implies that the person is aware of who he or she is and as a result, is better equipped to perform—each according to his or her abilities.

I've done a lot of self-exploration, whether through assessments such as DISC, Myers-Briggs, The Devine Inventory, StrengthsFinder, HOGAN, etc. Each takes time to complete, interpret and process and the value of doing so is worth it—especially as you move into Q3 and strive for excellence.

In a nutshell, here are some of my results:

- DISC – Dominance, Influence, Steadiness, Conscientiousness
- High D (dominance); profile – results-oriented pattern
- Myers-Briggs – ENFP – The Inspirer
- Clifton StrengthsFinder: Futuristic, Belief, Maximize, Activator, Connectedness

Jeff Caliguire, author, coach and speaker with whom I have worked, writes, "Contrary to what you may have heard, you can't do anything you want. However, you can do what you were uniquely created to do by fully accepting and engaging who you were meant to be. You find freedom."

As a CEO, husband and father, Jeff Caliguire's coaching integrated all parts of my life. It gave me the ability to really evaluate my dreams, gifts and skills…my mission; then gave me a written plan to move forward. It also inspired me to write my books.

Here is an expanded list of some of my talents reflected in the assessment results:

- I am good at influencing other people.
- I excel at strategizing, corporately, culturally and socially.
- I do well at visualizing and by that, I mean what I can visualize, I achieve.
- I am good at futurizing, meaning I can spot patterns easier than most others.
- I enjoy designing, in that I can put together an effective organizational model.
- I do well at conceiving not only my own ideas, but also recognizing other's great ideas and helping them work.
- I can create culture, rules and values that govern an organization.
- I thrive on excellence and challenge myself and others to this end goal.

I scored 100% on imagination (HOGAN) assessment. I thought this unusual. In the HOGAN results, I was surprised to score very low—or lower than I expected—on prudence. Perhaps this relates to my high score on mischievousness. Makes some sense, since my personal belief is that mischievousness—in a way—is the root of all courage.

This is where I am going with this…if you were prudent, you would just take a job at the USPS (post office) and you would be nice and secure. If prudence is a drive for security, then mischievousness may well be a sign of courage and ambition if you will. My comfort level with risk taking is pretty high. This is also true of my invitation for mischief.

If you saw my grandchildren, you would appreciate mischievous boys because it actually would be very scary if you had an overly compliant boy (or girl). That would be a problem. Mischief is somehow good. I encourage it. (Sorry parents.) Bottom line is it is not simply status quo.

Once again, I list my results not to focus on myself, but to give you an idea of what a two talent person might look like. I have a responsibility before God to invest these talents and to gain a return—to see them increase and develop, to bless others with them. I cannot bury these talents in the ground.

By the way…being a two talent CEO helps me to work on Main Street. Whereas five talent CEOs have to work on Wall Street!

A VERY PERSONAL ASSESSMENT – FROM SON TO DAD: A LETTER FROM KIRK SLAWEK

A relevant and pertinent assessment for me is the assessment of me from those I love most. In this case, I share a letter from my son, Kirk. Now, note that Kirk was not born until my 3rd Life Quarter, though I feel his remarks (shared at the onset of my Q4) are relevant here.

This what I learned…

LETTER FROM KIRK SLAWEK

The letter below was read at my father's induction into the Avodah Fellowship, which is awarded by Corporate Chaplains of America. My dad is the sixth recipient.

I was one year old when my father started FONA International, so I've lived my entire life in the shadow of this great company. I remember the excitement we all sensed when we moved from the smaller Northbrook (Illinois) facility to the cavernous 80,000-square-foot facility in Geneva (Illinois). Looking back on it, it seems like a blur.

Now that I have my own company, I realize how many things my father did that I took for granted. I remember how he started most of his meetings with prayer and did so without making people uncomfortable. I remember how he cherished the holiday meals when he and my mother joined all the FONA employees, even when the team had hundreds of people.

His willingness to trust God and walk away from his successful career to launch FONA is inspirational. That kind of calculated risk was unique, considering we were a young family with a toddler and a baby (me)! He and my mom moved in faith and God honored it.

Dad stood for Christ in the workplace he created and represented Him well, but he never pushed it. He was always available for anyone who had questions about the company or his faith. Dad's well-stocked library would never run low of recommended reading and he always gave away books to those who visited him.

How he led the company was how he led our family, with God and the scriptures at the foundation. When he built the facility in Geneva, I remember how we buried bibles in the foundation of every corner of the FONA building and in the auditorium. My father's company was literally built on the Scriptures!

A few years ago, Dad wrote a book on how to be successful in life and he often challenged me to read it. I told him I didn't have to because I had heard the audiobook my entire life! When I did finally read it, I realized I was right!

It cracks me up now when I often hear my dad's voice in my own as I lead my company. The values that he planted in me as his son were the same ones that he instilled in the team at FONA. He modeled radical generosity and genuine care for all of us. And he always believes in the best in people.

I'm so proud of my father's work and even though the FONA chapter of our story came to an end a few years back when he sold the company to McCormick, the story God is writing here on earth through him continues. And, for that, we are all grateful.

THOUGHTS FROM JOE

I did not know when I entered the board room at Kirk's office that he would accompany Mike Clowers and others from Corporate Chaplains of America. I certainly did not know about this letter until then. I was – and continue to be – moved beyond measure. The highest of honors from my son.

An assessment, I will always cherish.

LEADING BY INFLUENCE, NOT CONTROL – PURPOSEFUL ENTREPRENEURSHIP

Learning about myself and the viewpoints of others helps me to expand my common man abilities and be a successful two talent CEO, now as the CEO of my life. I learned – and continue to learn – what works and doesn't.

What I know is that control is the enemy of influence. So are narcissism, egotism and elitism. I imagine we each embody a tidbit or more of these descriptors and behaviors. Don't worry, we have allies in:

Excellence, Humility, Trustworthiness, Stewardship, Entrepreneurship, Connections, Insights, Determination, Tenacity, Relentless Pursuit of Excellence, Emotional Commitment, Gratitude, Overcoming Obstacles, Lifelong Learning, Giving…

In any case, the ally list trumps the enemy list.

The more informed we are about ourselves and the more willing we are to learn about ourselves, the nature of the work we do and the world we live in—the better. We are experiencing the rapidity of change and the impact this has on us at many levels. Much is shifting. Can we keep pace? I don't know. Can we surround ourselves with people, beliefs, values and faith to assist in traversing the journey? Absolutely.

In the book *The Nature of Success*, by Mac Anderson, founder of Successories and of Simple Truths, Mac wrote:

"I would think that there is no greater feeling than to look back toward the end of your life with a 'smile in your heart', knowing that many of your dreams came true, and that you made a positive difference in the lives of others."

GRADUATING TO Q3 — LIFELONG LEARNING

As you continue to Life's 3rd Quarter, the need and expectation—self-imposed and otherwise—is to pursue excellence. Excellence doesn't arrive. It is pursued. This comes through continuous learning throughout life. This is the place and space where you are—or should be—in the zone.

EVOLUTION VS. THE PRINCIPLE OF EXCELLENCE

Even if we appreciate the value of action and time, I am always amused by the way our society uses the word 'evolution' fairly often, but without thinking through the individual ramifications of the word. 'Evolution' suggests that any process, system, organism or organization or individual will improve over time by the simple passage of time.

Yet, our own human experience and observations shows the opposite. The reality is that with the addition of time without added stewardship inputs, things will always devolve and decay. This includes space orbits, habitats, bodies, processes, servers, computers, platforms, cars, etc.

Bringing it to our level, it includes each of us. Invest in YOU with your time and talents, rather than leave your opportunity for excellence to chance. Be a steward of yourself and of the people. Create your passage rather than wait for it. Be a seeker of learning and take advantage of learning opportunities provided to you.

For example, if you desire excellence in aspiring in business, you will want to pursue executive education programs. As a graduate and ongoing supporter of the University of Chicago, I learned about their Certificate of Business Administration Program. They called it UIC-CBAP. At FONA, we encouraged our employees at all levels to take the five-month course, classes taking place on Fridays and Saturdays. We made the education accessible and created awareness of the value of it. Then it was the employees' job to choose to show up—to grow. We had well over 125 graduates of that course and the skills and dedication contributed to the excellence of our people, products and our customers and factored into awards received for the brand and reputation we created.

There are a lot of people out there who don't realize what's available and it doesn't always cost anything. Learning is a click away on YouTube or at your local community college or art center or advertised workshops and seminars on Facebook or in the news.

Pay attention. Sign up. Go.

Step beyond borrowing your parent's dreams of the American dream, create your own.

Step into Excellence.

CHAPTER 3
LIFE'S 3ʳᴰ QUARTER – IN THE ZONE (EXCELLENCE)
TENETS OF BUSINESS AND LIFE

> "My Personal Mission/Adventure: Creating a culture of true wealth (which is God's Kingdom) through creating success, the relentless pursuit of excellence and exercising persistent faith and increasing commitment to reality."
> – Joseph James Slawek (JJS)

Now you know your industry, your job and a bit more about yourself. It is no longer work. It is what you do. Now you are in the zone. The question is: "How good do you want to become?" While you are always learning, it is now about execution. It's about excellence. No matter the industry or your role, this is the time that you will distinguish yourself. Will you become known as a great executive leader? A great salesman? A great entrepreneur? A great husband, father and community member?

I dreamt of my own business. I dreamt of being the best – to live that kind of excellence every single day. There is a better way and I know how to do 'it' better, so therefore, I must.

I love that love expands and I have more love with my children and spouse, scripture and Christian business principles.

My mentors included a continuation of people who had an imprint on my life across time. These were my leaders in faith, business and family. Also, if you can call it such, my 'mentors' also included the authors of great works regarding global trends, leadership, rapid technology change and multiple generations in the workplace.

At this juncture, I set a new standard of excellence. It sort of goes; failure, mediocrity, excellence, perfection. That's the spectrum. Excellence has a place. Excellence is the only thing for which to strive.

EXCELLENCE IS NEITHER PERFECTION OR MEDIOCRITY

EXCELLENCE IS THE PERSISTENT PURSUIT OF GROWTH

EXCELLENCE IS ALWAYS TO BE CHOSEN OVER GOOD ENOUGH

FAILURE IS A GOOD THING

A key word here is – failure. Many of us balk from it. I say, "Embrace it, because failure is the easiest to fix." You can fail and fix it, but you must call it what it was – a failure.

You can do good and most companies are busy doing good. A motive to standardize being good is that if you arrived at 'good', it may not take much to keep you at 'good'.

GOOD TO GREAT

Now, excellence requires the investment of just enough energy that it is clearly greater than average. You may think that at this point you must exert even more effort, more energy to become 'more excellent'. But be advised, you have to stop before reaching perfection as perfection cannot be reproduced.

At the end of the day, there is a huge difference between good and excellent. Most people quit at good. They are not going to build a successful or unique organization.

"When [what you are deeply passionate about, what you can be best in the world at and what drives your economic engine] come together, not only does your work move toward greatness, but so does your life. For, in the end, it is impossible to have a great life unless it is a meaningful life. And it is very difficult to have a meaningful life without meaningful work. Perhaps, then, you might gain that rare tranquility that comes from knowing that you've had a hand in creating something of intrinsic excellence that makes a contribution. Indeed, you might even gain that deepest of all satisfactions: knowing that your short time here on this earth has been well spent and
that it mattered."

- Jim Collins, Author of "*Good to Great: Why Some Companies Make the Leap... and Others Don't*"

THE CEO'S JOB

Across the years, I learned a lot about doing a good job as a CEO and sometimes doing a great job – reaching toward that excellence. Much of this wisdom ruminated and culminated in Life's 3rd Quarter.

I discovered a roadmap or blueprint about business and life and created the chart below to reflect it. The words are pretty descriptive, though I'll expand some.

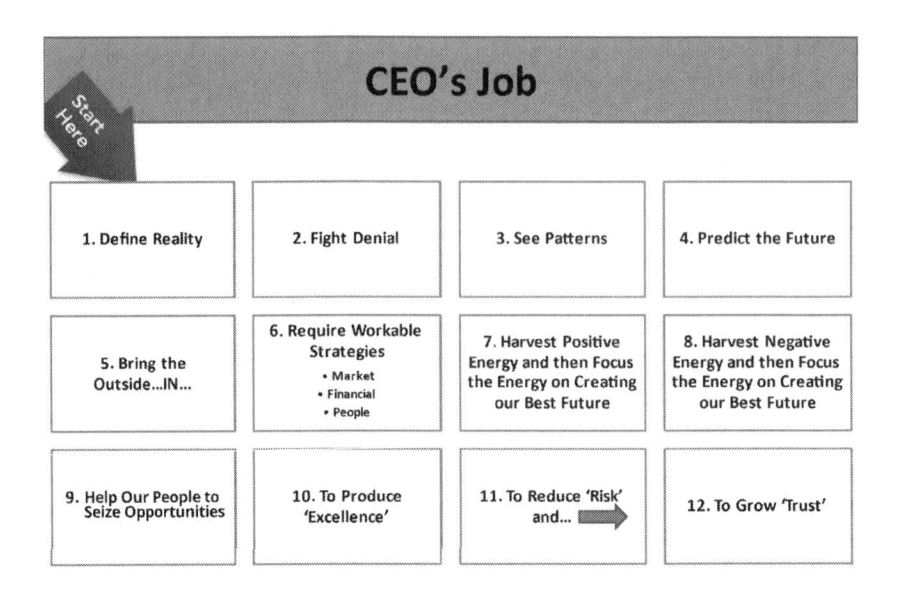

CEO's Job

Start Here →

1. Define Reality	2. Fight Denial	3. See Patterns	4. Predict the Future
5. Bring the Outside...IN...	6. Require Workable Strategies • Market • Financial • People	7. Harvest Positive Energy and then Focus the Energy on Creating our Best Future	8. Harvest Negative Energy and then Focus the Energy on Creating our Best Future
9. Help Our People to Seize Opportunities	10. To Produce 'Excellence'	11. To Reduce 'Risk' and... ⟹	12. To Grow 'Trust'

1. Define Reality – Answer and acknowledge what is real – what is or is not? What might be assumed vs. true? Know the difference.
2. Fight Denial – First identify – based on reality – what you are denying and own it. Then, prepare and do something about it.
3. See Patterns – Pay attention to what behaviors or results (or lack thereof) repeat or perpetuate. Look at the sequences leading to cause

and effect and call them out as patterns.
4. Predict the Future – With knowledge of 1-3 above, you have predictors of what is most likely to happen or be needed or to be thwarted for best outcome. Prediction is predicated on facts first.
5. Bring the Outside…IN… – Insular thinking will stagnate growth. New perspectives, insights and information – even if contrary – could propel it.
6. Require Workable Strategies: go to market, financial, people – The operative word is 'require'. Don't leave strategy to chance. Be deliberate about the leadership and management of strategic plans, objectives and actions.
7. Harvest Positive Energy and then Focus the Energy on Creating Your Best Future – Example: Develop a celebratory culture and one recognizing people, customers and application of best practices.
8. Harvest Negative Energy and then Focus the Energy on Creating Your Best Future – Example: Read the section below on Failing Forward!
9. Help our People to Seize Opportunities – Provide opportunity, training, mentoring and a performance-based culture and team environment.

And the above create these outcomes:

10. To Produce 'Excellence'
11. To Reduce 'Risk'
12. To Grow Trust

When I was in the zone conducting the CEO's job, I was happy and excited because I'd become skillful; and therefore, I was able to lead much more easily. When you place your awareness on these areas and learn from every occurrence, you will hit your stride. That stride leads to the clues of attaining excellence.

FAILING FORWARD

I have been the recipient of many accolades, many of which were a result of learning from making mistakes—and forging forward.

This I have learned to be true and I have been known to say it: "Every failure is a success." Bishop T.D. Jakes says it very well, "A setback is a setup for a comeback."

In some of my talks, I share the value of wounds and how the experience of wounds supersedes that of blessings. Accolades and awards are wonderful, yet you grow from wounds. Wounds come in many forms—being disappointed or mistreated or surprised. A differentiator affecting performance comes with learning to have the wherewithal to address the source of the wound and manage your personal perspective around it.

Forget and forgive? Perhaps. Or there may be a call to action, uncomfortable or not. The point is, move through it and move forward.

If there is a hiccup in learning, it is in doing nothing despite the fact that you have learned something. Look at mediocrity, but not necessarily from the standpoint of just choosing to be mediocre, but because in your striving for excellence you did not reach an intended outcome. What then? You give up? Sure hope not.

Own a failure. I see failure as no big deal because it's the easiest to fix. You just have to use the word 'whatever'. I failed this exam. I've failed to land this customer. I failed to communicate my point. I failed to show compassion…but..but…yada, yada. However, you can fix failure all day long.

Now, I will also say, "Do what you always did, get what you always got." In failing forward, the learning discovery is that there are many new beginnings to a different or more positive end. And maybe a five talent 'CEO' like Stephen Hawking said it best, "Intelligence is the ability to adapt to change."

PERFECTION IS IMPOSSIBLE TO REPRODUCE

Whenever I go for perfection, it is not a good place to be in. For starters it is a waste of time. There might be some one-time star alignment, but those more so happen when I am not trying.

As I have acknowledged, I am a common man. Never would I wager on being a perfect man. However, there are those magical (and elusive) moments of perfection or at least a sense of it. Yet, one of the things I know—that I have learned—is that perfection is not hard to produce, it is impossible to reproduce. Perfection is beautiful when it happens and striving toward it is motivating, but perfection simply cannot be reproduced.

I will give you an example of a perfect picture. So, picture this: I had a suit on for a board meeting. Mary doesn't see me in a suit often as I like to dress as my employees do—comfortably. Before we left home for the meeting she said, "Hey, let me grab a picture of you in front of the fireplace." She snapped it and sent it me to look at.

My reaction was, "Whoa! That's a great picture!" I never photograph well and that one was about perfect. It had the right lighting. I had the right posture and smile. The energy of my mood was obvious. It was a keeper. However, had we tried to re-enact that exact setting and pose the next day, well needless to say…it has not exactly been reenacted. (Maybe Mary has it framed somewhere.)

Perfection, when it happens, is very memorable and even motivating, but impossible to specifically reproduce. Strive only for perfection and you will fail. In the realm of failing forward, however, the argument every day is, "Am I going to be excellent?"

And that's what we should go for in all things. Excellence.

Understand that you're not going to have a perfect fourth quarter in life. Doing nothing is the only way to fail your 4th quarter, like if you decide to curl up by yourself and embrace being one of those 'old people'. If you decide to become a recluse that might be a failure.

The real choice is to step beyond mediocrity, apply the motivation toward perfection and realize the striving for excellence – and often achieving it – is about as picture perfect as it gets.

The real and deliberate piece is to make the decision between good and excellent.

So in Life's 3rd Quarter, while you are always learning, it is now about excellence. You finally have learned enough that you can apply yourself toward excellence…if you will. And excellence is just the rejection of being good.

THE 2X4 PRINCIPLE
– THE LAW OF RESPONSIBILITY AND THE PRINCIPLE OF EXCELLENCE

I have always known that we have been given individual gifts and talents. I have always known we have been charged with the responsibility to use these gifts and talents. The question for me was, "How does anyone know how to measure the results from using their gifts and talents?"

The Law of Responsibility says we are to double that for which we are given responsibility. At FONA our mission was to double our sales every four years. We gave each person a 2x4 block of wood as reminder of our responsibilities for the sustained growth of our customers, people and results. We applied this to our people, a holistic approach that demonstrates that unless you plan to grow or double or prosper, your life will not be as rich or as full.

You have the opportunity to create something valuable that did not exist before.

For your business, would you like a CEO that says and does double the size of the business and its returns over the next four years?

In your life, would you like a husband or wife who talks about making your relationship better by double?

As for me, I had the obligation—the responsibility—to double business results every four years and double the quality of relationships with key people in my life. And this will remain true throughout the rest of my time before joining my Creator (and I'm guessing after).

Everyone has unique gifts. And we are all on our way to being somewhere better.

In using your talents—you will appreciate the brush with excellence. It's not that you're going to succeed or it's not that you're going to be perfect. And it's not that you're going to fail. It's just that you reject that…that part of your life that is good…is good enough. You have committed to excellence.

We can do good. The difference, the real battle, is between good and great. Jim Collins, author of the massively acclaimed book, *Good to Great: Why Some Companies Make the Leap…and Others Don't*, writes that "Good is the enemy of great."

Am I going to settle for just being that good? Or will I choose to pursue excellence?

There's a big difference between good and great. It's the pursuit of excellence. Even better? Achieving excellence.

> "Excellence = hold self and others
> to the highest standards.
>
> How?
>
> Results expected."

There is a certain satisfaction that comes as you approach retirement. At the end of life's 3rd quarter, you can check some 'great' boxes. Here are a few I am blessed to be able to check:

- ✓ I've been successful.
- ✓ I have financial concerns out of the way.
- ✓ I have addressed image concerns.
- ✓ I now have a family and they are starting their families.

There are certainly numerous others with which I have been blessed, though perhaps I am most proud of those.

There is also the observation that you can stay too long rather than placing today and the future in others' capable hands. Think of some professional athletes, for example who came back one too many seasons with ensuing injuries and disappointing results.

I got us to Life's 4th Quarter—and now my 'job' is to craft a vision for my 4th quarter and what I will do, what I desire for those I love and a perpetuation of legacy.

The question I ask is: "How do I do this with excellence?"

RECOGNIZING AND APPLYING BEST PRACTICES

What works in creating a culture of success and excellence at home or work? The applicability of best practices for success is a reminder to focus on your own excellence no matter the endeavor.

From my book, *Ingredients for Success: 10 Best Practices for Business and Life:* I recommend the daily practice of:

1. Boldly yet compassionately tell the truth
2. Plan ahead but be ready for surprises
3. Know, develop, & use your unique abilities
4. Use your talents or you will lose them
5. Be ready for the accounting (*especially the BIGGIE; stairway to heaven*)
6. Invest your talents (faithfully) for maximum return
7. Aim for excellence not perfection (*perfection is hard to reproduce*)

8. Be strong & courageous
9. Redistribute unused talents and resources
10. Express gratitude to God and to others

INGREDIENTS FOR SUCCESS
10 BEST PRACTICES FOR BUSINESS AND LIFE

1. **BOLDLY** YET COMPASSIONATELY TELL THE **TRUTH**
2. **PLAN AHEAD BUT BE READY FOR SURPRISES**
3. **KNOW** DEVELOP & USE YOUR UNIQUE ABILITIES
4. **USE YOUR TALENTS** OR YOU'LL LOSE THEM
5. **BE READY FOR THE ACCOUNTING**
6. **INVEST YOUR TALENTS FOR MAXIMUM RETURN**
7. **AIM FOR EXCELLENCE NOT PERFECTION**
8. **BE STRONG & COURAGEOUS**
9. **REDISTRIBUTE UNUSED TALENTS AND RESOURCES**
10. **EXPRESS GRATITUDE TO GOD & OTHERS**

from Ingredients for Success: 10 Best Practices for Business and Life, by Joseph James Slawek, Kickstand Books 2013. All rights reserved.

"If you are faithful in little things, you will be faithful in large ones."

– Luke 16:10

God has best practices, too, for business and for life. He has something to say about how we conduct our daily lives. He has strategies for success in business and life. The reality is excellence in results is compounded when we apply proven best practices.

A NOTE FROM LUKE SLAWEK - EXCELLENCE

My dad created his own personal routines to succeed personally and professionally. He holds himself accountable and leads by example. I recognize more and more the brilliance of adhering to his own spiritual, physical, mental and emotional wellness daily. His track record is hard to comprehend so I've tried to summarize the observations that capture the perseverance someone would only see living or traveling with him:

> He leads his days with his health routines, walking 3 miles or more daily through weather, illness, injuries, surgeries, travel and as a priority among many time pressures. He also prays throughout the day frequently, no matter the company kept at restaurants or in his office. He takes vitamins and supplements and is a subject matter expert on each functional benefit. And he is always willing to consider better personal routines, like taking additional 30/60/90-day challenges. He has always been encouraging by his own adoption of disciplined routines, most of which others never start.

I have personally adopted and seek to grow myself through setting and sticking to personal routines – building my own formula of personal accountability to wellness. Dad is my example. Today, I have a similar series of routines and I find it is quintessential for me to 'show up' for the day. My kids have adopted simple routines that start upon waking, including pray, potty, stretch, personal hygiene and vitamins. Together, the kids and I are learning the value of consistency. The results at school, work and athletics validate our efforts.

> My dad's pursuit of excellence starts with himself when no one is looking or measuring, He does what he says he is going to do and it starts with him. I have come to believe this is the foundation from which the pursuit of excellence best starts.

LIFE'S 3RD QUARTER AUDIT – AN ACCOUNTING

There is always an accounting—daily, weekly, monthly, annually regarding how we have managed our responsibilities in business and personally. And eventually, there will be a final accounting from God—an external audit of your life and what you did with your talents.

Anyone in business is familiar with the idea of accounting—keeping track of earnings and expenditures, determining if a venture is profitable, seeing if a project is completed as it should be. Every successful business makes a habit of regular accounting of its work. Just working hard on something is not enough—we need to see results. When we are working, no matter what task we undertake, we need to keep the end in mind—and be ready for the accounting.

So in a sense, at the end of Life's 3rd Quarter, there's an audit. It might go something like, "Joe, you were an entrepreneur. You built a business to over a hundred million in revenue. You won Entrepreneur of the Year. You won the best workplace in America and …".

Getting that acknowledgement of "Well done, good and faithful servant" is important to me in my accounting, my audit. I'll probably put it on my tombstone, I hope, if I don't screw it up by then.

WHEN IS ENOUGH, ENOUGH?

Allow me to follow the idea behind the question, "When is enough, enough?" For example, if you are football quarterback Tom Brady and have won seven Superbowls or Aaron Rodgers with four MVP titles and both QBs are probably too old to be playing, well, when is enough, enough?

They are still great—and you may still be great at what you do.

Then, we can get into the 'what if' scenarios. In the quarterbacks' cases, "What if I break my arm and have limited mobility for life?" Or, if you are a CEO, what if your industry is overtaken by robotics or new innovations which quickly leave you bankrupt?

You can stay too long. That's the point. Best to walk away while on top. Prompt your 'audit' at the end of Life's 3rd Quarter and the BIGGIE accounting will follow at the conclusion of Life's 4th Quarter.

But how do you know when to walk away? That comes back to the calling you get in the Year of Jubilee.

THE YEAR OF JUBILEE

The Year of Jubilee is graduation from the third quarter in life. It is when you have eliminated debt and you have freedom in experiencing more fully, a new beginning.

As referenced in the Bible:

> The Year of Jubilee came every 50th year. It was one of releasing people from their debts, releasing all slaves and returning property to who owned it (Leviticus 25:1-13). The Jubilee year was also dedicated to rest. During this year, the Israelites were not supposed to reap or harvest. It was a time for people to return to their family and loved ones.

It's important to note that God owns everything. Anything he's given to us, such as resources, crops, etc., belongs to him. Therefore, the Israelites would dedicate this year of rest to him, acknowledging that God would provide for their needs.

For reference: (https://www.christianity.com/wiki/bible/what-was-the-year-of-jubilee.html)

There are three essential properties constituting the Jubilee Year (paraphrased):

- Personal Liberty: To be freed from the bonds of physical servitude.
- Restitution of Property: The means of fixing the price of real property; moreover, it should exclude the possibility of selling any piece of land permanently. The primary objective being the reversion of all hereditary property to the family which originally possessed it and the reestablishment of the original arrangement regarding the division of land.
- The Simple Life: Year of rest for the land (and therefore, for people).

Interestingly, we entered our 4th quarter at 49 years, the seventh of the seven year periods, which is the time to clean up your debts and pass things on to the next generation. I was in my 49th year of working. I made 50k per day in my industry. Heed the signs, right?

I heeded this biblical advice of The Year of Jubilee. Enough was enough. I did not want to become a roadblock to the next generations making their own mistakes. I wanted to release the reins to a new era. I felt I must pass along wealth in every definition of the word.

I am saying there's an important element in that there is always an audit that arrives at the end of the 3rd quarter. Definitely pay off your debt. I didn't become successful because of debt or borrowing and owing too much.

"If you will live like no one else, later you can live like no one else."
- Dave Ramsey

In an audit, maybe the results are good. Maybe they are not. We're not here to criticize anyone's third quarter of life. Maybe we're here to encourage everybody to celebrate their 3rd quarter. With the intel we gain from the audit, we'll see how we do in Life's 4th Quarter.

Let's get back to The Jubilee Year—the timing and how the time we have is or will be utilized in Q3 and Q4. Let's say you're a farmer in Ireland and you've been growing crops every seven of the seven periods and now you have to turn over your estate to somebody else. This story is set in Ireland to make a point. In Ireland you cannot inherit the farm until both parents die. (This aside, but I've heard it said that this may be a reason the pubs are so crowded in Ireland – not necessarily investing time in sowing and reaping??).

The son of the farmer has been taking care of his parents for years, while waiting to inherit the family farm. What's the problem with that, you ask? So, Dad dies at age 60, but Mom lives until age 80. Since the timing of The Jubilee Year has arrived and you are obligated Biblically to follow the principles, you are over a barrel. You've basically missed the 3rd Quarter of your life, whereas, you could have been excellent in taking life and a different trade or business in a different direction. The Year of Jubilee, just said, "Hey, enough's enough and on the seventh, seventh you will pass the torch."

(And I'm not being scripturally accurate, I'm being scripturally approximate.)

PROPER PLANNING

This is the time to turn things over. You may still be in a state of unprepared or you've prepared and may be ready—or in between. Well, it turns out that if you start working when you're 16 and you quit when you're 65, I think if my math is right, it's 49 years. And what a coincidence that this was the exact timing for my passing the so-called torch of my business.

In turning over the farm, the ranch, the business, whatever you have been doing, you should embrace when it is time to turn things over. Think of planning in your 3rd quarter for what will inevitably happen in your 4th—preparation for the ultimate handoff. Preparation for heaven.

Excellent preparation will give you ease of mind and will mitigate stressors for those surviving you and carrying on with greater ease – and even more excellence.

Below is a list of some high level, yet critical items, you'll need to address. Be aware of these, if not the leader of their completion. And make sure your team of advisors in tax, legal, bankers/investors, accounting, estate planning, medical and even emotional responders are in place, up to date and expected to be on the ready. Being on top of these things removes the sense of burden on you and the actual burden for your loved ones.

Create and keep current the following:

- Your Will
- Inventory of holdings
- Inventory of belongings
- Phone numbers of advisors – and ensure someone knows who each is and how to contact him/her.
- Funeral arrangements – typically the funeral home helps with obituary, but you may want to create your own and know or influence what will be printed and read about you.
- Info needed for taxes, probate, trust and other (seek advice)
- Ask your friends/family to honor communication preferences.

This is a short list. Your advisors will know more of what needs to be addressed and there is a lot of information online.

Of course, you must have the difficult talks with your children and other loved ones. The conversations are not fun and utterly necessary for peace of mind on all sides.

It is an interesting process to look back on the quarters of my life. There are things I have given up or lost. There are surprises. And, there are a whole lot of choices. Choices and decisions that have been made influence the trajectory of your life or flat out change it.

As is said by Red in the movie Shawshank Redemption, "Get busy dying or get busy living." I choose the latter, thank you.

LA LA LAND

As I've gone through or am still going through The Year of Jubilee and now living in the 4th quarter of my life, a lot of reflection is happening. I'm definitely still in the pursuit of excellence. I can try encapsulating what I think about or how I think – if that's possible – with a bit of what I took away from the movie La La Land.

I enjoy movies and La La Land is a favorite – a standout. I'm committed to watching it at least yearly and recommend you do the same. It is no wonder that it received multiple Academy Award nominations and wins.

Trying to describe La La Land is tricky because, as with life, it has many layers. I feel a good attempt was written by the Santa Barbara International Film Festival: "This is a beautiful film about love and dreams and how the two impact each other. Los Angeles is filled with dreamers and sometimes it takes a partner to make your dream come true." (www.sbiff.org – Sep 14, 2016)

The then, mostly unknown director (Damien Chazelle), wrote the screenplay in 2010. He is quoted in various media to have said, "…my idea was to take the old musical but ground it in real life where things don't always exactly work out and to salute creative people who move to Los Angeles to chase their dreams."

Sharing that again here is not a spoiler alert. Depending on how you view the movie, it could end happy or not so happy from your perspective. In my opinion it masterfully displays the clarity of what two people want professionally and the combustion that happens when faced with the love of two paths – the profession or the person in the La La Land characters' case. Can you have both or do you have to give up one or the other?

Having both doesn't always line up. In the movie the leads want what is best for each other. There is no interest in stepping on the other's dream. There is immense encouragement and support. Individual choices are made. Life moves along for each. Then, as only in the movies, we get a glimpse in a short sequence of scenes of what could have been had they chosen differently.

As a viewer, it made me uncomfortable albeit in a good way. You want them to get their respective dreams and you want them to be in love.

Coming back to 'real' life, in each quarter you have had or will have dreams and loves. La La Land prompts us to consider this: You'll be faced with the question, "If we all pursue our dreams, do we have to sacrifice our loves?"

Answer? Maybe, maybe not. Time will tell. Either way, you may receive more than you give up or be satisfied either way.

GRADUATING TO Q4 — WHAT MAKES AN 'EXCELLENT' 4TH QUARTER IN LIFE?

Okay, so I got us to the 4th Quarter—and now my 'job' is to execute the vision of what I desire for myself and for those I love and a perpetuation of legacy. It is also a good self-reflection (and decision) to know when to stay… and when is continuing to stay too long. And, I know how I am guided by Christian values and what I believe.

There are fundamentals in Life's 3rd Quarter to address prior to entering Q4, such as: making sure you don't run out of money; making sure you have insurance for the assisted living home; making sure you have a well-grounded business (okay, and personal) exit strategy; having your books in order to the 'T'; and ensuring your operations and people are attended to. And, perhaps most important, ensuring your children do not have to worry (as much) upon your passing.

Maybe those are all good things, but they're not excellent things. I even find some of them a little boring, perhaps because they are so obvious. A bigger driver leading to excellence is doing excellent things such as: estate planning so I'm not a burden on people; investing in the next generation (G2) leaders whether at the office, in high school or colleges; setting up a family office complete with a charitable arm; serving via the church and through or with the congregation of relationships gathered across time. Yes, and Mary and I plan some cruises and witnessing more of the world and its people.

And so what makes it excellent? I want to – no, I am passionate about – investing my time and other resources well. I WILL FINISH WELL!

SIGNIFICANCE

Even though I was a common man in life's 3rd quarter, I was able to shine as entrepreneur of the year, winning awards and setting records. All the things that you become excellent at during that 3rd quarter. I had success and now the focus turns to significance.

Significance is a bit better than receiving the gold 'retirement' watch. It is actually doing something significant. Take your rewards in this: maybe it is through paying for your grandchildren's education, doing charity acts, going to work for the church, being a good board member, being present for your wife and kids, investing in the future of youth. Whatever it is, you NOW must do something significant.

And I'm saying that if the beginning of the fourth quarter of life includes a successful end of the 3rd quarter, leave on top. And leave prepared and with a plan to perpetuate significance.

CHAPTER 4
LIFE'S 4TH QUARTER – GENERATIVE
THE TIME IS NOW
GENESIS...A NEW BEGINNING

"In the end, it is not the years in your life that count.
It is the life in your years."
- Abraham Lincoln

"Be selfless to be happiest."
- Joseph James Slawek (JJS)

"There is an earthly resume and also an internal resume.
Build both."
– JJS

In the Bible the scripture reads, "I tell you the truth, a grain of wheat must fall to the ground and die to make many seeds. But if it never dies, it remains only a single seed. Those who love their lives will lose them, but those who hate their lives in this world will keep true life forever. Whoever serves me must follow me. Then my servant will be with me everywhere I am. My Father will honor anyone who serves me."
– John 12:24-26 New Century Version (NCV)

What does this mean for me? It means that I had to prepare myself and the business for my departure and then let go. The aim is that others and perhaps something new grows from all I have learned in each quarter of life.

It is my time, our time, to be generative – to plant seeds for new generations as well as existing friends, family and many of the common men and women out there who want to and deserve to thrive and grow.

It is true that a grateful and indebted heart reflects a generous spirit. What better time to be generous with all that God has given me, than through my 4th quarter of life. As I now say, "One person's sunset is always another person's sunrise."

I dream of how I might be remembered. If we stay with the 'union" flow, I'm now the union steward. I wonder what my children and grandchildren will recall.

I love seeding the next generation, which includes time with my children, grandchildren and friends and more time with Mary. It also includes investing in generosity for those I may never know.

At this point, it is absolute that my mentor – my true guide – is God.

BEGINNING LIFE'S 4TH QUARTER...

It's one thing to begin the 4th Quarter of life as we covered earlier, the planning of which really starts toward the middle of the 3rd Quarter (if not sooner). This is where a timeout needs to be called to assess, okay, what now? Well, NOW, doesn't wait. We are in Life's 4th Quarter.

As Dr. Ken Blanchard, Chief Spiritual Officer of the Blanchard Companies, Inc., titled one of his books, *Don't Retire, Refire!* That's the right idea. Keep on keeping on! Watch out for the hiccups and the pitfalls of not having some level of clarity – if not full clarity – on how you will invest of your talents and time.

We will begin with a reflection on the flavorings of quality ingredients in business, which from firsthand experience, I can tell you overlap with successes in your life—however you may define the elements of 'success'. Though first, I would be utterly remiss, if the genesis of Life's 4th Quarter did not commence with thoughts from Mary.

A NOTE FROM MARY

What I know is that when Joe sets his mind to something, it will happen. I never imagined Joe leaving Food Materials, but it was the right thing, at the right time. He was on top as a salesman at his job and when he indicated it was time to start his own company I said, "We are going for this." We said it together and Joe took it and ran with it as is his innate ability to lead and forge forward. He knew he could do it and he was very clear he did not want to work for someone else his whole life. I had no doubt in my mind that this was right and it would work.

Interestingly, this decision to leave a well-paying job and begin FONA came very close to the same time we came to the Lord. That leap of faith led to our growth in our spiritual faith. I personally grew in faith in a way I didn't dream possible. We prayed – a lot.

This 'leap of faith', so to speak, paid off in FONA and in Joe's many successes. Those successes are also our family's successes. The kids and I were on site at the office often. When we realized that my skills and way of seeing people and situations complemented Joe's, I was quick to become a board member. I had a role at home and role in the business.

I have been asked how I maintained my sense of self as we prospered. There were so many demands on Joe's time and certainly my time in nurturing our children. The answer to that question is that I always wanted to be a mom. I am intended to be a mom. It is a bonus that I have business savvy and had coached and taught Physical Education gaining insight into people as well as business practices.

It is very important to me to be an example for my children as they continually grow personally, professionally and through their unique gifts and steadfast faith. The depth of my sense of self simply

> grew and continues to through God, my children and the honor it is to give back.
>
> As we are in Life's 4th Quarter, it is a whole new phase and an adjustment. My hope is that Joe will take a deep breath and enjoy it all. I am not suggesting he will go idle – not possible!
>
> "To whom much is given, much is required." – Luke 12:48
>
> We will continue this journey of blessing.

BACK TO JOE

It is pretty obvious—Mary is the foundation of making so much, so very possible. When I speak of grateful and indebted, well, thank you Mary.

So, I am no longer the CEO of FONA Inc., a multi-national company that creates flavorings for the food and beverage and pharmaceutical industries. Under my and my team's leadership, we amassed successes. Our growth was solid and steady as we expanded from a local company to an international one. We've also received the recognition of our peers—not just for our business success, but also for the culture we created.

FONA was named one of Chicago's 101 Best & Brightest Companies to Work, receiving Elite Status for the 15th year. We went on to the national level to receive the top award for mid-size businesses. We were recognized by *Inc. Magazine* for seven years running as one of the fastest growing private companies in the country. And, were also named Manufacturer of the Year by the Safe Quality Food Institute (SQFI). Topping off this summarized list of achievements, *Forbes* named FONA a Small Giant, One of America's Best Small Companies and *Fortune* named FONA #1 Best Small/Medium Workplace in Manufacturing & Production.

I was inducted into the Chicago Area Entrepreneurship Hall of Fame for driving growth that was five times the industry standard. And, I was named Ernst & Young Entrepreneur of the Year® for Manufacturing in the Midwest, a highly coveted and competitive award. I attribute these honors to operating with business and life principles intricately intertwined, knowing that honoring God and faith changes the lives of people.

All good stuff... I know that quality flavorings require quality ingredients. And success requires quality 'ingredients' as well. Beyond the achievements and awards, however, I may have learned more from the failures. Good news...I chose to fail forward in those circumstances. We made the best of all learned and corrected course as needed.

This is not just a business tenet. It is a tenet by which to live your life. There is a reflection of business principles in life and vice versa. <u>I will reiterate:</u> Business and life are intricately intertwined and honoring God therein and growing in faith changes the lives of people. I have the blessing of finding this out firsthand many times over.

In 2022, I was inducted as the sixth recipient into the 'hall of fame' of the Avodah Fellowship, an award given by Corporate Chaplains of America. Mary and I have donated to this wonderful faith-based organization across the years. The Hebrew word Avodah (ah–voe–dah) merges work, service to others and worship of God. Discovering Work as Worship is what Corporate Chaplains of America strives to build into company cultures all across the country. Corporate Chaplains of America is undaunted in sharing the hope of Christ and unleashing Avodah in the American workplace.

On their website there is a question: "What would it look like if work and worship merged for every believer?" Since at FONA, every day we strived for this, I realize why they may have selected me.

In any case, when I was asked to meet with them in person, I admittedly thought it would be for another donation request. I asked my assistant, Gina, to contact them and when she called me back, she pretty much told me I should go. I went and I am so glad I did.

A group of us met in our Nashville office where our son, Kirk, spearheads his business. I was presented with a beautiful trophy and honor. Kirk was with us and I had no idea he had been collaborating with the foundation to prepare for this ceremony. I was so touched and moved by the letter he wrote about me (see Chapter 2). Its meaning to me is immeasurable. Among many kind words and memories shared, he coined the phrase, 'radical generosity' too.

In Life's 4th Quarter, you are not at a stopping point. You are at a starting point. It's just a different starting point that with proper attention and intention can renew and reinvigorate.

GENESIS = GENERATIVE GENEROSITY

To me, Life's 4th Quarter focus is Generative. What are we trying to generate? Webster's Dictionary defines the word generate as having the power or function of generating, originating, producing, or reproducing. With my accumulated experiences and knowledge gained there is much I want to pass along to help pave the path for others.

Mary and I certainly believe in planting the seeds of growth in character, faith, career and life for new generations. It is a journey of blessing to generously provide resources, whether time, money, idea or access, which propel a person toward defining and capitalizing on their talents and having a rewarding life.

I lean toward a tendency to generate a good education for my grandchildren for example.

Generosity does lead to legacy and a new beginning. I take radical generosity as doing what is well above and beyond. More so, giving of time, talent, wealth or other riches is the right and good thing to do.

It's interesting that the word 'generosity' begins with the word G-E-N-E-. This is the same root word of genesis. Genesis, as with the first book in the Bible, is a beginning.

- GENESIS -

word-forming element meaning "birth, origin, creation," from Greek genesis "origin, creation, generation."

https://www.etymonline.com/word/-genesis

Want to know how to give 1 million dollars away? I'll tell you how. Give a dollar. After you do that, give 10 dollars. After that, give 100 dollars. Then give 1,000 and then 10,000 and then 100,000 and work up to that 1 million. Exercise that muscle. Generosity takes regular exercise.

I've paid off all my debts and I've retired from working and now I can invest in generosity. It's not about an ending. It's providing opportunity and inspiration to seed the next generation. Most of the people think that generosity is separating, giving something away and it disappears. But real generosity is seeding. It is planting the genes for the next. It's placing seeds in ministries that can grow and make changes in people.

I have a memory that influenced me – that placed a seed – in my distinct interest in generosity. It stems with my Grandpa Masura who assembled me, my sisters and my cousins – about 10 of us – when we were around 5-8 years old. Grandpa was probably age 56 when we visited him. He was the Union Business Agent (imagine that) of his local union. He and Grandma had a color TV (these were Lawrence Welk days), nice furniture, a chandelier lamp – some things I saw then as the accoutrements of wealth.

On this particular day, Grandpa Masura came home with an entire toy board. If you remember 'back then' department stores had displays with toys pegged across. You could pull a toy from the board to purchase. Well, Grandpa bought the entire board of Mickey Mouse battery projectors. Basically, these were projectors from which you could project Disney character images onto walls or a ceiling. Each one of us assembled got to select one for ourselves. We didn't even have to share!

We each found a place in my grandparents' bedroom, laying side by side on the bed or sitting together on the floor. We pulled the drapes and we began our light show. We laughed and played and the entire experience was topped off with awe at such generosity from Grandpa. It's never left me, this memory. It was the most generous of riches I could conceive of. A very pure gift. The richest act – super-abundance –

more than enough for everyone.

    A 4th quarter dream for me is to seed that sort of memory for my children and grandchildren and my eventual great-grandchildren. Call it legacy or a slice of immortality. In addition to memories, I dream and love to seed new opportunities for family, co-workers and those I don't even know. Not to ask them to do what I have done, but just because I can. With Christian principles and faith guiding me, I must. And it gives me joy.

> "I have learned that people will forget what you said,
>
> people will forget what you did,
>
> but people will never forget how you made them feel."
>
> - Maya Angelou

A NOTE FROM LUKE SLAWEK – CONTINUING THE LEGACY

Today I find myself laying the seeds of foundational values with my kids, which I learned directly from my dad's role modeling. We built our own family values. We set goals. We seek to serve others. And, we hold excellence as our measurement of success.

The conversations at our kitchen table are long-term oriented and I know it stemmed from my parents doing the same. My parents have been extraordinary role models in the value of being future focused and starting everything important with the family.

It is common that people recognize my last name and begin pouring their hearts out about the transformational impact my parents had on them. The testimonies have inflection points that changed their lives and future for the better. They almost always have attributes that make them better people, spouses, parents, leaders and community members. They give the credit to my parents' selfless and kind investments in them. Their mentorship has impacted innumerable people wide and far, living on in mentors that cascade through those they influence.

A CONTINUATION OF OUR TALENTS

Bob Buford's book, *Finishing Well*, shares statistics about the longevity—or lack thereof—for those who leave what they knew, like a job or title, without knowing what will fill any gap that is real or perceived in their heart and soul. Without a plan of action and some passion, your lifespan could actually shorten. I'm not risking that.

So when I use the word generosity, it's not finishing. It's what things do we want to begin. So whether we're generous to our grandchildren by leaving them a college fund, the genesis of a good education—or whether we give to a ministry or whatever else—it's because we think they can change lives or have new beginnings.

So the fourth quarter of life is about being generative and displaying generosity but not endings, if you will. What are we going to seed in that 4th quarter?

As I reflected on the parable of the talents, one business truth clearly stood out to me: we are asked to be faithful stewards and to double what has been given to us. I have long noticed that some of the leaders I've observed often had that abundance of success not only in their finances, but in their relationships as well. I've always wanted to understand the reasons. Perhaps this is why I was so enthralled by Jesus' teaching in Matthew 25.

Responsibility is an obligation. We are each to use our talents responsibly. In preparation for Life's 4th Quarter, we did a ton of estate planning and we did a ton of passing along. God challenged me in the area of stewardship, but he also clearly spelled out my responsibility to double what he's given me and helped me to understand the reward for doubling, the penalty for failing and the accountability in all of the cases.

From a business perspective and as a leader, I came to understand that our responsibility at our company was to double our revenue and results every four years, hence the concept 2x4. The concept follows for me, my family, friends and colleagues for each of us to double our personal results every four years at each of our levels of talent and ability.

As with entering the world of entrepreneurship and enterprise value creation…you have the opportunity to create something valuable that did not exist before! In Life's 4th Quarter!

I have often called myself a two talent CEO. Since retiring from FONA, I no longer have the title of CEO. I embrace the continuation of being the CEO of my own life. Now, it is my opportunity to strive toward being a five talent Good and Faithful Servant for God, Family, Community and much more. I do not expect perfection, but I do expect of myself a perpetual striving for excellence.

This will include how I distribute my faith, enjoy every moment with my family and continuously learn more about myself. Growth does not stop in Life's 4th Quarter and generative generosity can expand.

A CONTINUATION OF YOUR TALENTS: YOUR CHECKLIST

I encourage you to think about how you move along your path of significance and contribution in Life's 4th Quarter. Whether on a napkin or a formal document, I am a proponent of 'the list' – that is, a checklist to remind me of what is important and the need to focus to achieve or maintain momentum. It is not necessarily a 'to do' list, as it shouldn't feel like work. Simply, it keeps you on point in living in a way that is fulfilling. Consider the following…

Start the day by asking:

- How do I want to feel?
- What will I do for myself and in the service of another?
- Who needs to hear from me?
- Is there something left undone requiring my attention?

Keep front and center the intention to:

- Be generous.
- Be charitable.
- Show love – a phone call, a hug, kind words.

- Take a moment (or many) to reflect on all for which you are grateful.
- Pray.

Complete your checklist. Maybe some days you can check each box, maybe not. At least you are checking in and being intentional about what will fill your days with what you design.

WHAT'S NEXT?

As you get into Life's 4th Quarter you realize, hey, there's only a certain time period left. I'm healthy now, though longevity may or may not happen. So Life's 4th Quarter is an excellent opportunity to assess what lights you up and what you will do with your light. What and who do I want to take care of? Myself included.

In this 4th quarter, I think there's a realization that you need to redistribute your emotions on people and entities. And it especially puts the time clock a little more center in your mind. It's more about the game clock than the scoreboard. So far in my 4th quarter I've learned that it is perhaps a tougher adjustment than I thought to not be the guy in charge. I no longer have employees to guide and lead and my children are effectively leading vastly on their own, though I do hope they will always come to me with questions and needs. I'm in a more private time of life and a lot is shifting and changing.

Relationships are essential to me and I enjoy having many of them at once. Some go very deep. Some are more in the shallows. If you look at a square napkin you can spend your 'entire box' on 2 people, Mom and Dad for example. If you divide that napkin into 4 parts, you can spread your time and talent across more people. It doesn't mean you don't go deep. It's the same amount of relationship energy expended – and received, based on your nature. An introvert may prefer fewer people, an extrovert more.

Whether introvert or extrovert, we cast our net to nurture those relationships and people we want and need to keep closest. And we can feed our need for interaction and diversity by situationally reaching out to the many. How we cultivate and maintain relationships is up to each of us.

I want to focus on things that are important to me, one of which is giving, I have that generous soul if that makes sense. My plan includes giving to institutions and to people who will never be able to give back to me. Many or most of these people I will never meet.

EMOTIONAL REDISTRIBUTION

Emotions are redistributed in each quarter and more specifically in the 4th Quarter. At this point in time, you realize I'm spending my time on 200 plus people and their families, but maybe I'm not spending enough time on my own family. And I think for most people who have been in my kind of positions it's true—you are more likely solving a problem for an employee or a customer.

There will be serious problems. And if your family doesn't have a serious problem, you may not be interacting that much. And because you like fixing things and solving things…where am I going with this? Well, it is on those things you will spend your time. Perhaps often unaware of how much your family needs that time—problem or not.

Mary and I have a favorite 'adoptee', Connor. I give him advice that is healthy and good for him. I tell him the honest truth even if it may be hard to hear or to comprehend. I sometimes contemplate if I could ever have had this nature of conversation with my own kids. What I realize though, is at this stage in my life, I have perspective…maybe even some wisdom. And I find it much easier to impart it due to my life experiences and all that I have been blessed to learn.

REDISTRIBUTION OF 'THINGS'

A lecture I am prone to give to my kids is on what I title, "Beware of the Tyranny of Things." What I mean is that you do not want 'things' to rule you. That ruling, like that of a dictator, can be oppressive. Ideally, everyone should be aware of such 'tyranny' in Q3 – before they have too much excess to address in Q4.

Success may allow the purchase of a boat, car, jet ski or second house. That is nice at first glance, however, the ripple effect – or consequence – is then the management of a mortgage or insurance payments, maintenance and all of the basic upkeep. In the case of material items, you may find an un-used accumulation like the three bikes in the garage, Grandma's China (or three sets of it) or collections of boxes in storage spaces with labels like figurines, model airplanes or prom dresses. You know what I mean. Have you missed those things? Did you perhaps forget you had them?

When I warn of the tyranny of things I say, "This in the spirit of love, but one more thing doesn't seem like a lot, but it is one more thing that takes your attention at the expense of a person who could be receiving that attention." The more things you have the greater the tyranny.

I think moving 'things' along is part of The Jubilee. If your possessions have little meaning, do you really need them? Create some space, physical space and mental and either sell or give what truly is not serving a purpose. Is there a daily jubilee? Can there be? Yes. Be charitable. I mean if I haven't used that bike in the garage because the tire has been flat for a year, I am unlikely to become inspired to ride it anytime soon.

SIMPLIFYING IS GOOD. SIMPLICITY TOO.

How much do I actually think soaks into my children from my pulpit regarding the tyranny of things? I would imagine, time—in their lifetime—will tell. I'm not sure I believe in sitting on a cloud while in heaven, but if so, I may be peering down and mumbling, "Told ya so."

> Whether it is the redistribution of emotion or the redistribution of things, it is the redistribution of the clutter (or your clutter) that allows you to have more of what is most important—your care, your passing on what you know, your love and the best is…witnessing your loved ones share what they learned or heard from you…with those they love, which means you already love them too.

A message may not stick in the moment of the telling, but it might stick later and get repeated. Maybe my kids won't read this book, but they have heard the 'audiotapes' their entire lives.

In Life's 4th Quarter talents can still be redistributed. Personally, I want mine to be recycled in the most positive ways—to and through others.

Imagine a LIFE reflecting these values:

- In pursuit of excellence
- Being a steward
- Forward thinking – study trends, competitors, consumer appetites, other industries, leaders and their behaviors (good or not so good)
- Integrity
- Honesty
- Ethics
- Loyalty
- Long-term relationships

God willing, this will be so.

GRATEFUL AND INDEBTED

> "Be thankful in all circumstances, for this is God's will for you who belong to Christ Jesus."
>
> – Letter from Apostle Paul: 1 Thessalonians 5:18 (NIV)

I must express my gratitude to God and to every person who has touched my life. I am grateful and indebted for much and to many. The list could become a scroll, though I'll begin with my gratitude to God for his ever-present blessing, protection and prosperity. For the many gifts, talents, events, responsibilities, authorities, successes, failures, problems, losses, gains, changes, weaknesses and strengths which he gave me and those I love in the course of our development.

Each year at FONA we celebrated Thanksgiving with food and cheer and even bonuses to demonstrate our gratitude. We created a booklet to which anyone could contribute reflections on what they are grateful for. I cherish those booklets. When we were closing out of our primary role with the company, Mary and I decided to show our indebtedness. With a few hundred employees, it was important to us to be equitable and to share in the many riches in our hearts and souls. We decided to demonstrate this through gifts to each employee of $2500 per year served and a total of 7.1 million total.

Not sure I've ever felt wealthier in my life than to be able to give. Many lives were changed and impacted that day. Mine too.

The credit for our success belongs to God for his abundant help, blessing, protection, mercy and providence throughout our history, our today and into our future. In turn, I seek first to honor him in all our activities.

For you…please be generous with your gratitude and appreciation. Be generous with your time and resources. Be generous with your forgiveness. Be generous with your kindness and goodwill. Be generous with your patience, love, hope and joy and most important, be selfless in order to be happiest. My deep gratitude and indebtedness to each and all of you.

As said, each foot in front of the other requires discipline. Until the day I meet my Creator, the finish line will still be inches away.

Experience enjoyment. If you don't, the talents you were given and those you have accumulated will still be redistributed. Use it or lose it, right? I am delighted with what I have learned over the years and that which I have set in motion to stay in motion.

I'll continue to think about and create significance in business and life, because I'm not at a stopping point, WE are at a starting point. It's just a different starting point.

Another new beginning.

FANFARE FOR THE COMMON MAN

"Whatever you do, work at it with all your heart, as working for the Lord not for human masters, since you know that you will receive an inheritance from the Lord as a reward.
It is the Lord Christ you are serving."
– Colossians 3:23-24

"God is not unjust. He will not forget your work and the love you have shown Him as you have helped his people and continue to help them."
– Hebrews 6:10

As for fanfare, I DO want to be remembered as a common man. I've thought to myself, "What song would I want played at my funeral?" There's a great song by Emerson, Lake & Palmer. The band was classified as a progressive rock band and were perhaps ahead of their time.

Perhaps I love this piece of music because I resonate with being a common man with big dreams.

The song, *Fanfare for the Common Man*, is fully acoustic. There is an iteration of it on YouTube where the band is in a grand football stadium. The field is packed with snow. The big tom toms drums open and the synthesized 3-tier organ and a slaying electric guitar groove with beats that cause you to stand up and let the sound pulse in your heart.

You can also listen and watch another version at this link: https://www.youtube.com/watch?v=Xe49IF7IySw – on Jay Leno, circa '93 or search Fanfare for the Common Man on YouTube.

Obviously, I love that song. It is triumphant and almost like a bugle call reflective of time on earth and a quest toward those gates where I hope to hear, "Well done, my good and faithful servant." I also hope that my family will heed my wishes of being buried in a tuxedo. I figure that is an appropriate way to meet God in person for the first time.

Perhaps I am not a prototypical example of the community of people I am around. I just happened to be the oldest of eight kids from the Northwest side of Chicago. There's also a part about my being a common man, going back to the early stage from my family. My father was alcoholic. We lost Mom and my dad much too soon. I attribute these experiences as instrumental in my success.

We learned to put the fun in dysfunctional. Lord knows when I was little, in my teens and college, life was riddled with dysfunction. But somehow or another, that ability to navigate dysfunction became and is still a skill set. As you will—or are—discovering, something is always dysfunctioning. If you can hold your own…you are learning something that's pretty precious.

So there was no elitism in our family. No room or interest in that. Therefore, I believe in non-elitist meritocracy. You may ask, "How does (or did) a common man make it in this elitist dominated world?"

Gently, yet as a force—for good, this I know.

I think of it as, I'm just a common man who had to work part-time throughout grammar school, high school and college. And when that 1st quarter of life was over, this common guy was very happy that I just had one job to work full time at as opposed to being the student and all the things that come with that part. I was sort of like, education is done. Great!

But I turned out to be a lifelong learner of things I really cared about. So at the end of life's 2nd quarter, you can come back to acknowledging I was nothing special except I seemed to take learning very seriously and I also outworked my peers.

To go along with the common man theme there is another hint that I'm a common man. At the end of the 3rd quarter and business success, this common man showed up in the form of being able to—and simply being connected to—my employees. I connected because of my nature. I don't play out airs and rank. Believe me, if I did, I would hear about it.

I had a somewhat irregular upbringing in the responsibilities I assumed and was open with my colleagues with that story. It was important to me to fit in with them at our workplace and in our fun and celebrations. I came from a working and production background and had—still have—distinct appreciation for hard work, mental acuity, kindness and all the value based on faith.

I cared also about connecting with the elite in industry, though I did not cross the line into elitism. I stayed true to myself. And to those around me. Maybe that is one of my biggest accomplishments.

And then finally, I think when you get him—the common man—to Life's 4th Quarter, it is the measure of that man in part, to give back to his fellow common man. I think to myself, "Aren't there hundreds of common men you could help? I have nothing against windmills, recycling, clean energy, etc., but it strikes me as a Don Quixote-like metaphor for global warming. You're jousting with windmills.

Our family's charitable fund recently gave to Judson University. The contribution helps fund young men and women who are the first in their family to attend college. Inadvertently, giving these scholarship participants an opportunity may just develop the forward thinking and wherewithal to address what we face together. In the meantime, one by one, we change the trajectory for people—one by one—and maybe then, collectively.

I may never meet the person whose life I touched. And in my lifetime, I may not meet my last grandchild. It is a humbling thought. It is also heartwarming, knowing my footprints march on.

My greatest 'fanfare' is and will eternally be, the fanfare of the successes and significance of—and within—every one of my loved ones. As my family grows and grows in faith, I hope so will grow the seeds I have planted in minds, hearts and souls.

As I reach those 'pearly gates', the comment I pray to hear is, "Well done, my good and faithful servant."

Perhaps the best question I may hear is, "What would Dad do?"

EPILOGUE
MOVING FORWARD...

Life's 4th Quarter is not a closing, but it is a beginning. I, thus, felt it apropos to share a prayer:

>Lord, you ask us to seek your wisdom.
>
>Lord, I seek your wisdom in all areas of my life, and at all times in my life.
>
>I seek your will, your wisdom and your Kingdom.
>
>Let thy will be done.
>
>Amen.

>"But seek first the Kingdom of God and His righteousness, and all these things shall be added unto you."
>— Matthew 6:33

>"Let this be written for a future generation, that a people not yet created may praise the Lord."
>— Psalm 102:18 (NIV)

ACKNOWLEDGEMENTS

I look forward to Life's 4th Quarter with my wife, Mary, and our continued journey. Thank you for every moment of our days together and for your divine hand in guiding our family and often me, with such grace. Thank you also for your generous letter in this book and your perpetual support of my endeavors.

With deepest love, I acknowledge my children for blessing me and expanding my life experience beyond measure. As your families grow, my heart continues to expand.

Thank you to my parents and to my siblings. You were and are a foundation of the creation I am.

This book would be but an idea if it were not for Kristin Andress who served as my editor, prompter and guide during the process of sharing my experiences and wisdom from my life's quarters. Thank you, Kristin.

Thanks also to Bill Butterworth who served as editor of my first book, *Ingredients for Success: 10 Best Practices for Business and Life.* I selected excellent excerpts from the content to enhance and improve Life's 4th Quarter.

To Gina Capuani I am grateful for all you do for me personally and for our business. Your personality and gifting are an asset to our family name and reputation.

There are many to acknowledge on my path through life. I hope as life has transpired that I have demonstrated my gratitude. Please accept it now. This gratitude continues.

And it is with humble reverence, that I thank God. Without You, nothing is possible. I hope this reflection of life assembled in a book, is but one step closer to hearing, "Well done, my good and faithful servant."

Joe Slawek will tell you that he is at a 'new beginning', the 4th Quarter of his life. He has a vision for his coming days including: to be generative, meaning plant seeds for new generations; to be generous by providing many dimensions of opportunity; and, to continue his personal journey in his faith.

From sweeping floors to extracting vanilla to leading sales, Joe rose through the ranks at Food Materials Corps. That is, until he arrived at a veritable fork in the road – a keen desire for autonomy in taking the actions and risks necessary to start his own business and eventually redefine the flavor industry.

That business, Flavors of North America (FONA) founded in 1987, became FONA International, creating and producing flavors and complete market solutions for many of the largest food, beverage and nutritional companies in the world. FONA's core values drove a pursuit of excellence and the fostering of customer partnerships and employee relationships. His employee base of over 225 people and their families enjoyed a culture encouraging innovation, learning and rewards.

Perhaps as the oldest of 8 children in his family, he had an original leg up in understanding dysfunction and how to traverse and thrive through it. Joe is a common man who has achieved extraordinary things. FONA was named one of Chicago's 101 Best & Brightest Companies to Work, receiving Elite Status for the 15th year. They went on to the national level to receive the top award for mid-size businesses. They were recognized by *Inc. Magazine* for seven years running as one of the fastest growing private companies in the country. They were also named Manufacturer of the Year by the Safe Quality Food Institute (SQFI). Topping off this summarized list of achievements, *Forbes* named FONA a Small Giant, One of America's Best Small Companies and *Fortune* named FONA #1 Best Small/Medium Workplace in Manufacturing & Production.

Joe was inducted into the Chicago Area Entrepreneurship Hall of Fame for driving growth that was five times the industry standard. He was named Ernst & Young Entrepreneur of the Year® for Manufacturing in the Midwest, a highly coveted and competitive award. Joe operates with business and life principles intricately intertwined, knowing honoring God and faith changes the lives of people. With recognition, Joe was inducted as the sixth recipient into the 'hall of fame' of the Avodah Fellowship, an award given by Corporate Chaplains of America, undaunted in sharing the hope of Christ and unleashing work, worship and service in the American workplace.

Joe is the author of *Life's 4th Quarter,* released in 2023. His book *Ingredients for Success: 10 Best Practices for Business and Life* was released in 2013. In his personal life, he is an instrument-rated private pilot flying his VisionJet, values outdoor activities and is actively committed to his family, his church and to community service.

He is a graduate of the University of Illinois-Chicago, where he met his wife, Mary. They have three adult children and seven grandchildren. Joe is CEO and Chairman of Slawek Family Holdings (SFH) and leads focused efforts dedicated to securing the future for the next generation of successors.